GROW IN LOVE
FIFTH CLASS/PRIMARY 7

VERITAS

Grow in Love Series
Published by
Veritas Publications
7–8 Lower Abbey Street
Dublin 1, Ireland

publications@veritas.ie
www.veritas.ie

ISBN 978 1 84730 846 7

This textbook has been approved by the Irish Episcopal Conference. It is in accordance with the Catholic Preschool and Primary Religious Education Curriculum for Ireland (2015) that was approved by the Irish Episcopal Conference and granted the Decree of Recognitio by the Holy See in 2015.

10 9 8 7 6 5 4 3 2 1

Veritas books are printed on paper made from the wood pulp of managed forests. For every tree felled, at least one tree is planted, thereby renewing natural resources.

Writer: Elaine Mahon
Original illustrations: Norma Prause Brewer
Art direction & design: Lir Mac Cárthaigh

See page 149 for copyright acknowledgements.

A catalogue record for this book is available from the British Library.

Printed in Ireland by Boylan Print Group, Drogheda

Welcome to *Grow in Love*

Dear Families,

Welcome to *Grow in Love* for Fifth Class/Primary 7. This year we begin by reminding the children that God knows and loves them unconditionally. They can come to know God better by reading the Bible, through which God speaks to us. We teach the children how to look up Scripture references. We also introduce them to the prophets Isaiah and Jeremiah.

The apostles and other disciples gradually came to know Jesus better by listening to the stories he told and by observing how he treated people. The children will hear the parable of the Workers in the Vineyard and a story about Jesus healing a man with a paralysed hand. At first the apostles thought that Jesus was a prophet, but they eventually came to see that he was the Messiah whom God had promised. After the Resurrection, when they saw and recognised the Risen Jesus, they knew that he was God.

Abraham, Moses and Samuel responded to God's call, as did Mary, who agreed to be the mother of Jesus. The apostles responded to Jesus' call to help him to carry out his mission. Today, people from all walks of life respond to God's call in different ways – people who are single or married, ordained or members of religious orders.

Advent is a time of waiting for Christmas. It mirrors the time when Elizabeth and Zechariah, and Mary and Joseph, waited for their babies to be born. We help the children to see that Christians all over the world celebrate Christmas in different ways.

We teach the children that our conscience is God's voice within us that guides us to recognise right from wrong. Sometimes listening to our conscience means having to make difficult choices.

We tell the children that the Catholic Church calls us to work for justice for all – that includes migrants and refugees who are fleeing from unjust situations, and people who are suffering from poverty and other forms of injustice. There are many examples of people who spend their lives working for justice for others.

We follow the last journey of Jesus to Calvary and celebrate his Resurrection. Before he ascended to heaven, Jesus promised to send the Holy Spirit to his followers to help them to live as he had asked them to. The Holy Spirit comes to us today in Baptism and Confirmation. We explore the Sacrament of Confirmation in detail.

We examine the diocesan and parish structure of the Church and we reflect on the roles of bishops, priests and deacons. We introduce the children to the Sacrament of Holy Orders.

The children will hear the story of the disciples meeting the Risen Jesus on the Road to Emmaus and recognising who he was when he broke bread with them. This is our starting point for an examination of the structure of the Mass, which mirrors what happened on the road to Emmaus.

In the seasonal lessons we focus on life after death, the customs associated with remembering St Patrick, Lent, devotion to Mary as it is expressed through Marian shrines and artistic images, and the Jewish faith.

We continue to provide opportunities for the children to participate in vocal and meditative prayer and we help them to be aware that, when they pray, God is always listening to them.

Throughout this book you will find activities that you can do each week with your child to support the work that the teacher is doing in school. We encourage you to take this opportunity to teach your child about the faith that you chose for him or her at their Baptism. We hope that, with the support of the teachers in your school and of your parish community, this programme can help you as you journey with your child to 'grow in love' of God and of others.

THIS WEEK IN SCHOOL

You are invited to think about:
- What you know about God
- How much God loves you
- How and when you can pray to God

KEY WORD

Christian: The word 'Christ' is a special title given to Jesus. It means 'Anointed One'. Christians are followers of Christ.

THEME 1: GOD IS ALWAYS WITH US | LESSON 1

God Knows Us and Loves Us

WE GET TO KNOW ONE ANOTHER BETTER ALL THE TIME

We spend a lot of time together, inside and outside of class, so we know a lot about one another. But there will always be things we don't know about one another.

This year we will get to know one another even better. As we do, we will notice the ways in which we are different and the ways in which we are similar. God calls us to respect the differences we see in each other and to accept every person for who they are, because everyone is special. Everyone is a child of God.

GOD KNOWS US AND LOVES US BEST OF ALL!

Christians believe that, above anyone else, God knows us best. God knows all there is to know about us, even things we don't know about ourselves. And, knowing all these things, God loves us completely and absolutely. God loves us with an everlasting love. No matter what we do, God still loves us.

Psalm 139 in the Bible describes this love that God has for each one of us. Here are some verses from that psalm:

Psalms 139:1-6, 13-16

Lord, you have examined me and you know me.
You know everything I do;
from far away you understand all my thoughts.
You see me, whether I am working or resting;
you know all my actions.
Even before I speak,
you already know what I will say.
You are all around me on every side;
you protect me with your power.
Your knowledge of me is too deep;
it is beyond my understanding ...

You created every part of me;
you put me together in my mother's womb.
I praise you because you are to be feared;
all you do is strange and wonderful.
I know it with all my heart.
When my bones were being formed,
carefully put together in my mother's womb,
when I was growing there in secret,
you knew that I was there –
you saw me before I was born.

JOURNAL EXERCISE

- Write a letter to God on the first page of your new Religious Education journal, sharing with God your thoughts about starting this new school year – your hopes, fears, dreams and worries. You may also like to include any prayers that you have for yourself or others.

FOR MEMORISATION

Lord, you have examined me and you know me. (Psalms 139:1)

RECALL THE SONG: 'CLOSE TO YOU'

- The composer of this song says that he wants to be close to God. Recall his words:

  But you are always close to me,
  Following all my ways.
  May I be always close to you,
  Following all your ways, Lord.

- In what ways can we get close to God?
- The composer also says he wants to 'follow' the Lord's ways. Can you think of how someone might do that?
- Talk about the times when you feel closest to God. What helps you to feel close to God?

PRAYER KEEPS US CLOSE TO GOD

The composer of the song 'Close to You' wanted more than to know *about* God: he wanted to be *close to* God. This points to the difference between knowing something in your head and knowing it in your heart. We can know all about God and still not be close to God. We can only grow close to God through prayer – through talking to God and listening for what God may be saying to us – and through loving others.

THINK ABOUT IT ...

- At what times during the day will you, as a class and in your own private time, pray, and therefore stay close to God this year?

THIS WEEK

The children took time to get to know one another better and to learn new things about one another. Throughout the year, they will get to know one another even more. They will also get to know more about God. We reminded the children that God already knows and loves each one of us. We can talk to God in prayer. This helps us to stay close to God.

Rocks can remind us of God. Rocks are strong and they resist wind and rain. The psalms in the Old Testament often speak of God as a rock, because God is all-powerful and God's love for us is everlasting and never changes. Read the poem 'Prayer Rock' together.

Prayer Rock

I'm your little prayer rock
and this is what I'll do.
Just put me on your pillow
'til the day is through.

Then turn back the covers
and climb into your bed,
and, whack! your little prayer rock
will bump you on the head.

Then you will remember
as the day is through,
to kneel and say your prayers
as you intended to.

Because your heavenly Father
cares and loves you so,
he wants you to remember
to talk to him, you know.

AT HOME

DID YOU KNOW?

God calls each and every person to be close to him. Prayer helps us to grow closer to God.

TIME TOGETHER

Respond and Share

Decide on one time and way in which your family can pray together. That may be at Sunday Mass, or a prayer before a meal, or an action like blessing yourselves with holy water when leaving your home. Write your suggestion in your Religious Education journal. Then share what you have written with your parent or guardian.

Pray Together

Pray together the verses from Psalm 139 that are on the second page of this lesson.

Be Prayerful

Try to say a prayer each day – to thank God for your blessings, to praise God, to ask for forgiveness, to ask God for help for yourself or someone else, or just to share the thoughts you are having with God.

THIS WEEK IN SCHOOL

You are invited to think about:

- How words can both hurt and heal
- How God speaks to us through the Bible
- How the Bible offers us wisdom for our daily lives

KEY WORDS

Chapter: Each of the books of the Bible is divided into chapters, just like a novel is divided into chapters.

Verse: The chapters in the Bible are subdivided into verses. Each verse usually consists of one or a number of sentences.

Scripture references: Scripture references refer us to specific chapters and verses in the Bible. They are usually written in this form: Matthew 3:13 (name of book, chapter, verse).

THEME 1: GOD IS ALWAYS WITH US | LESSON 2

God Speaks to Us through the Bible

WORDS ARE POWERFUL

Words have the power to hurt as well as to heal. Hurtful words can be just as painful as a physical injury. Hurtful words can be spoken, or sent through a text message or by social media. On the other hand, words can also bring healing, encouragement and love.

JOURNAL EXERCISE

- Imagine one of your close friends is being bullied and they come to you and tell you about it. Make a list in your Religious Education journal of all the words or phrases you might say to this friend to comfort them and to show them you care. Also, name the adult(s) whom you would advise them to talk to about it.

GOD SPEAKS TO US THROUGH THE BIBLE

As Christians, we believe that one of the ways in which God speaks to us is through the Bible. The Bible is the Word of God. Even though the words in the Bible were written thousands of years ago, they still have meaning for us today, and they always will. That is why Christians love and respect the Bible. We can learn from the Bible and it can help us to grow closer to God and to other people. If we follow the teachings in the Bible, we will live happy lives.

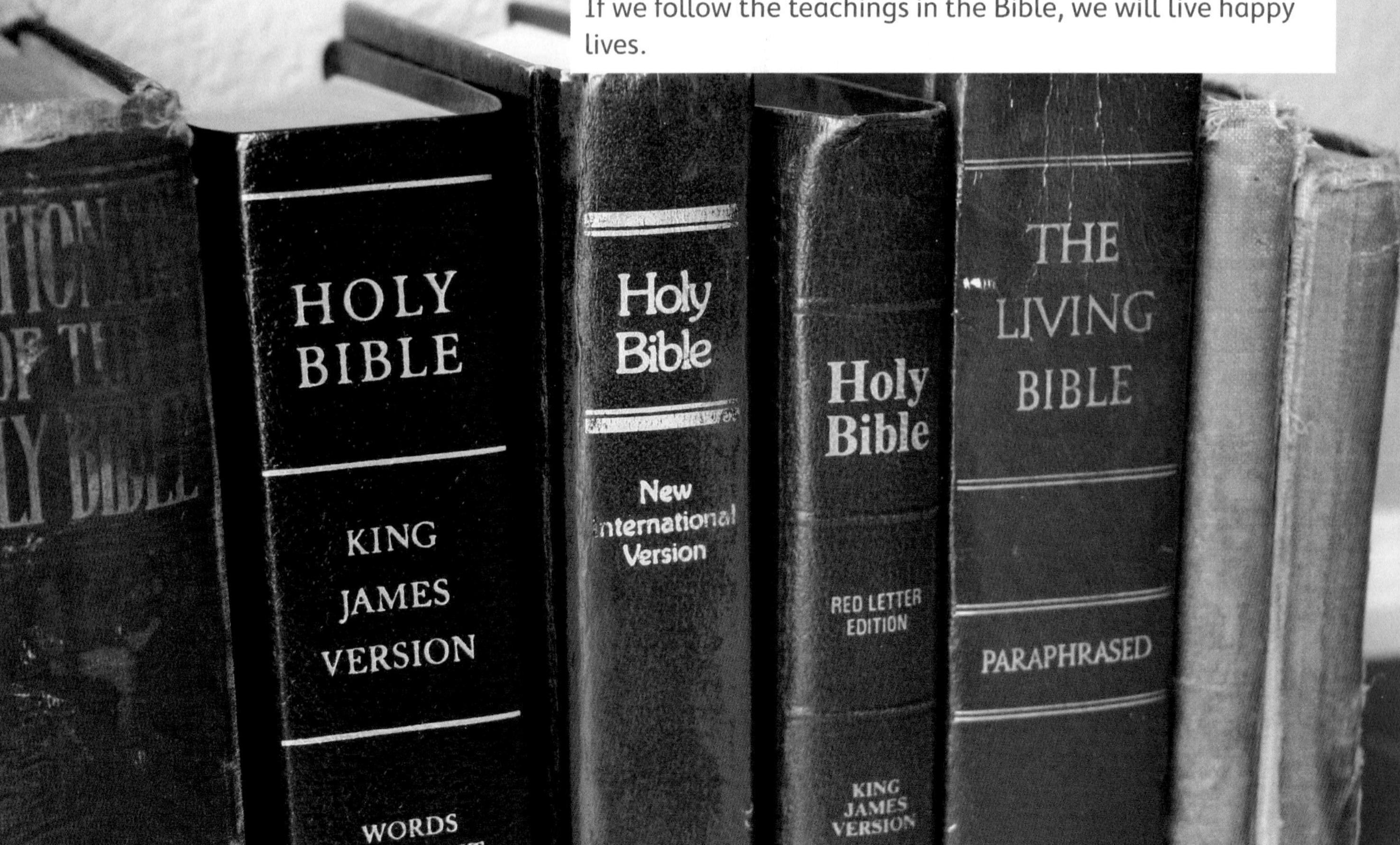

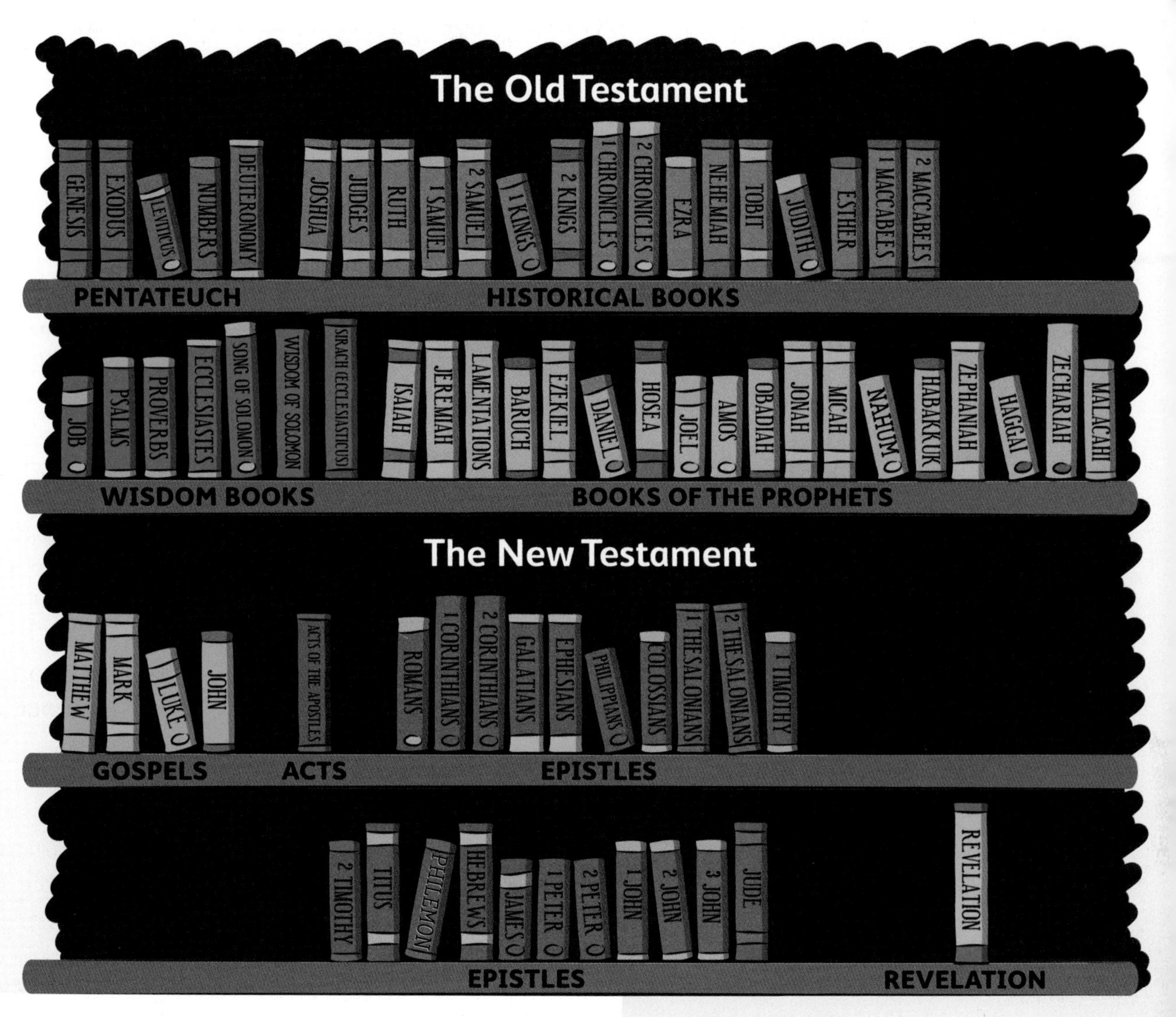

WORDS OF WISDOM FOR OUR LIVES

The Bible is also known as Sacred Scripture. Every part of Sacred Scripture contains words of wisdom that can help us to live our lives in the way that God desires. Answer the following questions to help you recall what you already know about the Bible:

1. What does the Old Testament tell us about?
2. What does the New Testament tell us about?
3. Name the four collections of books in the Old Testament.
4. Name the four parts of the New Testament.

SCRIPTURE REFERENCES

A **Scripture reference** has three elements:

- The name of the book
- The **chapter** of the book
- The **verse** (which usually consists of one or a number of sentences)

For example, Matthew 3:13: the name of the book is Matthew; the chapter number is 3; the verse number is 13.

FOR MEMORISATION

Do for others just what you want them to do for you. (Luke 6:31)

BIBLE SEARCH/JOURNAL EXERCISE

- Work in pairs. Each pair will choose one of the Scripture references listed below.
- Locate your chosen Scripture reference in your Bible.
- Write the verse into your Religious Education journal.

1. Sirach 7:18
2. Proverbs 16:16
3. Ephesians 4:29
4. Exodus 20:12
5. Galatians 6:9
6. 1 John 4:20
7. Romans 12:13
8. 1 Thessalonians 5:11
9. Luke 6:31
10. John 13:34
11. Ecclesiastes 4:9
12. Colossians 3:13
13. Proverbs 24:17
14. Romans 12:18

THINK ABOUT IT ...

- What do you think our class would be like if we all lived according to these verses from the Bible? Would it change things? In what way?

THIS WEEK
The children reflected on how words can be very powerful. Words can be used to hurt as well as to bring comfort. The Bible contains many words, which are organised into verses, chapters and books. The words in the Bible can have a strong effect on our lives because God speaks to us through the Bible. The Bible is the Word of God.

Pray this prayer together:

Loving God,
thank you for the gift of your Word in Sacred Scripture.
May we always take your words to heart,
and use them to make good choices.
May your Holy Spirit help us to turn away from using
words that cause hurt or unhappiness to others,
and instead use our voices to help people feel good.
We ask this in Jesus' name. Amen.

AT HOME

DID YOU KNOW?

Even though the Bible was written a long time ago, its message is still as meaningful for people today as it was when it was written.

TIME TOGETHER

Chat Together
Chat about how the words we use to our family, friends and even strangers can have a powerful impact. By choosing our words carefully, and always treating others as we would like them to treat us, we can live happy lives and bring happiness to others, just as God intended.

Respond and Share
Think about a time when someone helped you to feel better by using kind and loving words. Write about this in your Religious Education journal. Then share what you have written with your parent or guardian.

Be Careful
Be careful with the words you use when talking to and about others. Try your best to use words that show support, encouragement and love.

THIS WEEK IN SCHOOL

You are invited to think about:

- What the prophets have told us about God
- How God calls each of us to speak up for what is just and right
- How you can answer this call in your day-to-day life.

KEY WORDS

Covenant: An agreement. God made various covenants with his people, which are recorded in the Bible.

Prophet: A person who speaks on behalf of God.

THEME 1: GOD IS ALWAYS WITH US | LESSON 3

The Prophets Speak the Word of God

RECALL THE STORY: 'THE TREASURE HUNT'

- Why did Ade not want to be on a team with Oisín, Samantha and Sadhbh?
- What did Oisín do when Miss O'Flannagan gave him the pack with the instructions?
- What did Sadhbh suggest they do after they had opened the first clue?
- Why was Ade unhappy with that suggestion? What did he say to his three teammates?

KEY PEOPLE IN THE OLD TESTAMENT

The Bible tells the story of God's relationship with his people down through the ages. The Old Testament tells us about God and his people before the coming of Jesus. These are some of the key people that we meet in the Old Testament: Adam and Eve; Noah; Abraham and Sarah; Moses; Joshua; the prophets.

THE PROPHETS

God sent **prophets** to remind the people of the **covenant** God had made with them. Prophets are people who speak on behalf of God. There are many stories about prophets in the Old Testament. Some of the prophets even wrote books in the Old Testament.

PROPHET IN THE SPOTLIGHT: JEREMIAH

Jeremiah was about twenty years old when God called him to be a prophet to the Israelites. This is how that moment is recalled in the Book of Jeremiah:

The Lord said to me, 'I chose you before I gave you life, and before you were born I selected you to be a prophet to the nations.'

I answered, 'Sovereign Lord, I don't know how to speak; I am too young.'

But the Lord said to me, 'Do not say that you are too young, but go to the people I send you to, and tell them everything I command you to say. Do not be afraid of them, for I will be with you to protect you. I, the Lord, have spoken!' (Jeremiah 1:4-8)

Jeremiah then went and did as God asked. He spoke out against those who had forgotten about the one true God and who had put their faith and trust in foreign kings and strange gods. Many people were angry with Jeremiah – angry at the way he spoke and angry at what he said. At one stage, Jeremiah was thrown into a deep well and left to die, but even from the depths of the well he continued to speak out.

On one occasion, Jeremiah stood outside the Temple, as God had asked him to, and told the people what God wanted them to hear. This is what he said:

> 'Change the way you are living and stop doing the things you are doing. Be fair in your treatment of one another. Stop taking advantage of aliens [strangers], orphans and widows. Stop killing innocent people in this land. Stop worshipping other gods, for that will destroy you. If you change, I will let you go on living here in the land which I gave your ancestors.' (Jeremiah 7:5-7)

There were times when Jeremiah wished he had not been called by God to be a prophet. But deep inside himself, he knew he was doing the right thing in speaking God's Word.

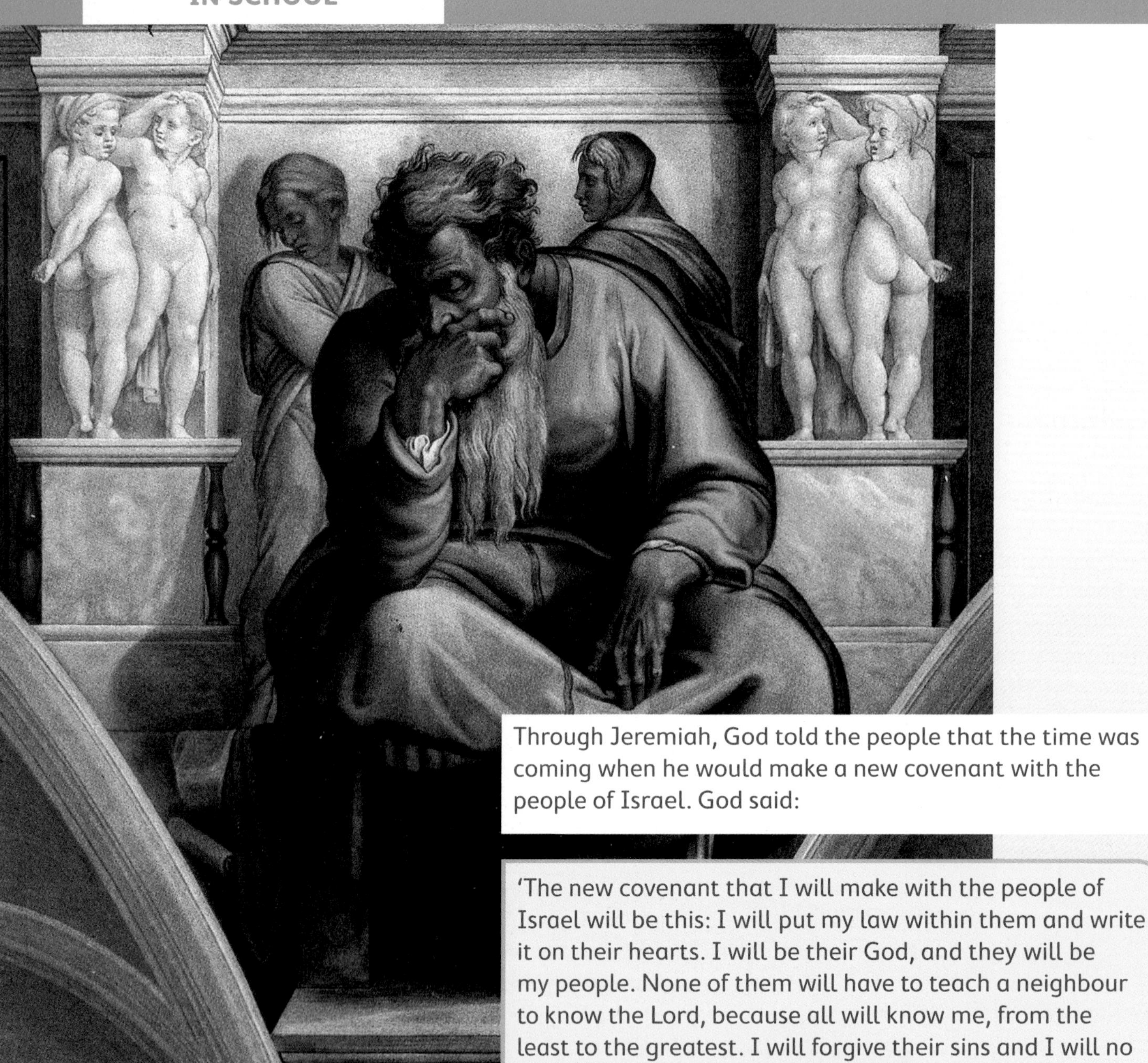

Through Jeremiah, God told the people that the time was coming when he would make a new covenant with the people of Israel. God said:

'The new covenant that I will make with the people of Israel will be this: I will put my law within them and write it on their hearts. I will be their God, and they will be my people. None of them will have to teach a neighbour to know the Lord, because all will know me, from the least to the greatest. I will forgive their sins and I will no longer remember their wrongs. I, the Lord, have spoken.' (Jeremiah 31:33-34)

Jeremiah is one of seven prophets painted by Michelangelo on the famous ceiling fresco in the Sistine Chapel in Rome

- How old was Jeremiah when God called him to be a prophet?
- What was Jeremiah's reaction to being called?
- What did God say to Jeremiah to reassure him?
- What message from God did Jeremiah give to the people when he stood outside the Temple?
- How do we know that Jeremiah's life as a prophet was not easy?
- Where did God say he would write the new covenant that he would make with the people of Israel?

FOR MEMORISATION

'Change the way you are living and stop doing the things you are doing. Be fair in your treatment of one another.' (Jeremiah 7:5)

JOURNAL EXERCISE

- Is there anything in the story of Jeremiah that you think might help you in your own life? Write about it in your Religious Education journal.

AT HOME

THIS WEEK

We reminded the children that, in the beginning, God created a world where everything and everyone was good. Then people turned away from God's goodness and began to sin. But God didn't give up on them. Instead, God sent the prophets to speak on his behalf and call people back to the covenant; back to his love. The children heard the story of the prophet Jeremiah, who continued to preach God's Word despite opposition. They also heard about Martin Luther King Junior, whom many people would regard as a modern-day prophet.

Read the poem 'Jeremiah the Prophet' together.

Jeremiah the Prophet

'Not me, Lord,' he cried, 'I'm too young and too small.
Choose another, someone strong, to answer your call.'
The Lord knew why he had set Jeremiah apart.
Appearances mean nothing – God looks at the heart!

Despite his fears, Jeremiah answered the call
To be a prophet and share God's message with all.
Facing much opposition and against all the odds,
He preached, 'Change your ways and don't believe in false gods.'

Despite all the challenges, he kept on with his task,
Preaching of God's faithfulness and the covenant that will last.
Jeremiah persisted, drawing strength from above,
The fire in his bones transformed this prophet of love.

Many people regard Martin Luther King Junior as a modern-day prophet

DID YOU KNOW?

When the people neglected the covenant that God had made with them, God sent prophets to call the people back to him. The prophets were messengers from God who spoke the Word of God.

TIME TOGETHER

Respond and Share

Reflect on a time in your life when you did the right thing, the thing that God would want you to do, even though it may have been difficult. Write a paragraph about that time in your Religious Education journal. Then share what you have written with your parent or guardian.

Pray Together

Loving God,
give us the courage to remain true to you and to your Word.
May we be inspired by the prophets to always stand on the side of what is right.
We ask this through Jesus, our friend. Amen.

Be Courageous

When you have a difficult decision to make, take time to think about what to do. It may take courage to do the right thing, and the right thing may not always be the popular or easy thing to do. Ask the Holy Spirit to guide your decision.

THIS WEEK IN SCHOOL

You are invited to think about:

- The Parable of the Workers in the Vineyard
- What it means to be generous
- Ways in which you can be generous towards others, especially towards people who tend to be forgotten or left out
- How you can help build the Kingdom of God in our world

KEY WORDS

Kingdom of God: It is also called the Reign of God and the Kingdom of Heaven. This does not refer to a specific location or to any physical place. Instead, it refers to the type of world that we create when we live according to the values that Jesus taught. The Kingdom of God exists wherever people live together in a community of justice, peace and love.

Parable: A story that is used to teach something important. Jesus often told parables to teach people about the Kingdom of God.

THEME 2: JESUS | LESSON 1

The Parable of the Workers in the Vineyard

RECALL THE STORY: 'A STORY OF LOVE AND GENEROSITY'

- What happened to Thomas? Why did he have to spend so long in hospital?
- How did Fiona and her mother show Thomas that they loved him?
- What did Thomas do to show his mother that he loved her?
- What big surprise did Fiona get a few weeks after her brother returned home from hospital? How did that make her feel?

JESUS TAUGHT USING PARABLES

Jesus came on earth to teach people about what God is like and to tell people about the **Kingdom of God**. Jesus often used stories called **parables** to help people to understand what the Kingdom of God is all about. One of Jesus' parables was the Parable of the Workers in the Vineyard.

Now read the first part of the parable as it is told in the Gospel according to Matthew.

The Parable of the Workers in the Vineyard – Part 1 (Matthew 20:1-7)

'The kingdom of heaven is like this. Once there was a man who went out early in the morning to hire some men to work in his vineyard. He agreed to pay them the regular wage, a silver coin a day, and sent them to work in his vineyard. He went out again to the marketplace at nine o'clock and saw some men standing there doing nothing, so he told them, "You also go and work in the vineyard, and I will pay you a fair wage." So they went. Then at twelve o'clock and again at three o'clock he did the same thing. It was nearly five o'clock when he went to the marketplace and saw some other men still standing there. "Why are you wasting the whole day here doing nothing?" he asked them. "No one hired us," they answered. "Well, then, you go and work in the vineyard," he told them.'

THINK ABOUT IT ...

- Think about how each of the five groups of workers might have felt as they waited to be hired.

Now read the second part of the Parable of the Workers in the Vineyard ...

The Parable of the Workers in the Vineyard – Part 2 (Matthew 20:8-16)

'When evening came, the owner told his foreman, "Call the workers and pay them their wages, starting with those who were hired last and ending with those who were hired first." The men who had begun to work at five o'clock were paid a silver coin each. So when the men who were the first to be hired came to be paid, they thought they would get more; but they too were given a silver coin each. They took their money and started grumbling against the employer. "These men who were hired last worked only one hour," they said, "while we put up with a whole day's work in the hot sun – yet you paid them the same as you paid us!" "Listen, friend," the owner answered one of them, "I have not cheated you. After all, you agreed to do a day's work for one silver coin. Now take your pay and go home. I want to give this man who was hired last as much as I gave you. Don't I have the right to do as I wish with my own money? Or are you jealous because I am generous?"'

And Jesus concluded, 'So those who are last will be first, and those who are first will be last.'

FOR MEMORISATION

Jesus said, 'Those who are last will be first, and those who are first will be last.' (Matthew 20:16)

THINK ABOUT IT ...

- In the parable, the workers who were hired later in the day were paid the same as those who were hired early in the morning. What do you think about that? What does that say to you about the generosity of the vineyard owner?

GOD'S GENEROSITY

The vineyard owner represents God. God always gives people more than they deserve. God's generosity knows no limits. Everyone is treated equally in the Kingdom of God.

THIS WEEK

The children heard the Parable of the Workers in the Vineyard. Because of the generosity of the vineyard owner, the workers who were hired last were paid the same as the workers who had been hired early in the morning. The actions of the vineyard owner give us an insight into God's love, mercy and generosity. God acts with generosity towards all – the first and the last alike. One lesson that we might learn from this parable is to think about how we can be more loving and generous towards others, especially towards people who tend to be forgotten or ignored.

Talk about how the pictures on this page show people living by the values of the Kingdom of God. Which values of the Kingdom of God are being illustrated in these pictures?

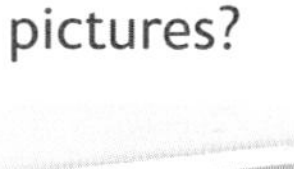

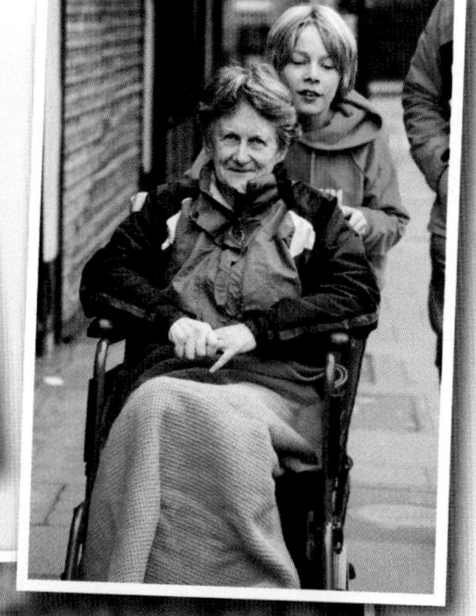

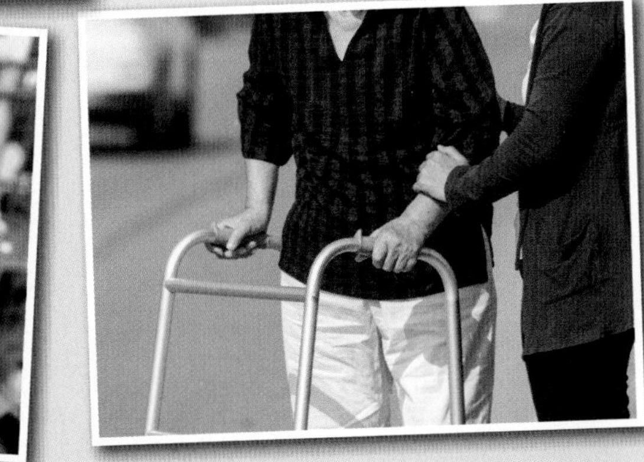

DID YOU KNOW?

We can help to bring about the Kingdom of God in our world when we are kind and generous towards others, especially towards those who tend to be forgotten or ignored.

TIME TOGETHER

Respond and Share

Do you remember a time when you saw someone you know living by the values of the Kingdom of God? Write about it in your Religious Education journal. Then share what you have written with your parent or guardian.

Pray Together

Each time we pray the first four lines of the *Our Father*, we ask God to help us make his kingdom come on earth as it is in heaven. Pray the first part of the *Our Father* together now.

Be Generous

Be on the lookout for people who always seem to be forgotten or 'last' – people who are less popular than others, who are made fun of, or who don't have as much as others. Treat everyone as equals, as God does, and so make the Kingdom of God come about.

THIS WEEK IN SCHOOL

You are invited to think about:

- The Third Commandment
- Jesus' action of healing a man on the Sabbath in light of the Third Commandment
- Times when you put the needs of others before everything else

KEY WORDS

Sabbath (Shabbat): The Jewish holy day, which Jews observe as a day of rest.

Synagogue: A place where Jews gather to worship God.

Pharisee: A member of an ancient Jewish movement that is mentioned many times in the New Testament.

Serenity: The feeling of being calm and peaceful.

THEME 2: JESUS | LESSON 2

Jesus the Healer

WISDOM VERSUS KNOWLEDGE

Wisdom is different than knowledge. Knowledge means knowing the facts about a situation. Wisdom means understanding what those facts mean. A person needs wisdom in order to know what to do in difficult situations. Wisdom comes with experience; it comes as we get older and as we experience different situations and learn from them.

THINK ABOUT IT ...

- Recall a time when you showed wisdom in a particular situation. How did you come to have such wisdom? How did having this wisdom help you?

THE THIRD COMMANDMENT

For Christians, Sunday, the Lord's Day, is a holy day. The Third Commandment teaches: Keep the Lord's Day holy. This Commandment is based on the following passage from the Book of Exodus. **Sabbath** is the name Jews use for their holy day, or day of rest.

God spoke, and these were his words ... (Exodus 20:1, 8-11)

'Observe the Sabbath and keep it holy. You have six days in which to do your work, but the seventh day is a day of rest dedicated to me. On that day no one is to work ... In six days I, the Lord, made the earth, the sky, the seas, and everything in them, but on the seventh day I rested. That is why I, the Lord, blessed the Sabbath and made it holy.'

JOURNAL EXERCISE

- Think about the ways in which Christians keep Sunday, the Lord's Day, 'holy'. Record some of those ways in your Religious Education journal.

JESUS HELPED PEOPLE

Jesus always helped whenever he saw someone in need, even on the Sabbath. Now read a story about Jesus healing a man on the Sabbath.

Jesus Heals a Man with a Paralysed Hand (Matthew 12:9-14)

Jesus left that place and went to a **synagogue**, where there was a man who had a paralysed hand. Some people were there who wanted to accuse Jesus of doing wrong, so they asked him, 'Is it against our Law to heal on the Sabbath?'

Jesus answered, 'What if one of you has a sheep and it falls into a deep hole on the Sabbath? Will you not take hold of it and lift it out? And a human being is worth much more than a sheep! So then, our Law does allow us to help someone on the Sabbath.' Then he said to the man with the paralysed hand, 'Stretch out your hand.'

He stretched it out, and it became well again, just like the other one. Then the **Pharisees** left and made plans to kill Jesus.

- What question did the people ask Jesus at the beginning of the story?
- What example did Jesus give them of a situation where they might have to do some work on the Sabbath?
- What was wrong with the man whom Jesus healed?

FOR MEMORISATION

The Serenity Prayer
God, grant us the **serenity**
to accept the things we cannot change;
courage to change the things we can;
and wisdom to know the difference.

THINK ABOUT IT ...

- Think about some things you could do to help others on the Lord's Day, and by so doing keep it holy?

JOURNAL EXERCISE

- Imagine that you are the man whom Jesus healed on the Sabbath. Write a diary entry in your Religious Education journal that the man might have written before he went to bed that night.

AT HOME

THIS WEEK

The children heard a story about Jesus healing a man on the Sabbath Day. Some people believed that Jesus was wrong to do this, because the Third Commandment taught that the Sabbath was to be a day of rest, free from work, and they regarded healing a person as work. Jesus had the wisdom to know that it may sometimes be necessary to put the needs of others first. By helping the man, Jesus was putting the man's needs first, and by doing so he *was* keeping the Sabbath Day holy.

Pray this prayer together:

The Serenity Prayer

God, grant us the serenity
to accept the things we cannot change;
courage to change the things we can;
and wisdom to know the difference. Amen.

DID YOU KNOW?

Jesus taught us by his words and by his actions that it takes courage and wisdom to do the right thing, especially when other people think you are wrong.

TIME TOGETHER

Chat Together

Do you think Jesus was right to heal the man on the Sabbath Day? Why or why not?

Record and Share

Do you remember a time when someone you know put the needs of another person above all other things? Write about it in your Religious Education journal. Then share what you have written with your parent or guardian.

Be Wise

Take time to think first before you act when you have a difficult choice to make. Pray for wisdom and courage to do the right thing.

THIS WEEK IN SCHOOL

You are invited to think about:

- Jesus as the Messiah whom God promised through the prophets
- Your own answer to Jesus' question, 'Who do you say I am?'
- How you can grow closer to Jesus by learning more about him

KEY WORD

Messiah: A Hebrew word meaning 'anointed'. Jesus was the Messiah whom God promised through the prophets.

THEME 2: JESUS | LESSON 3

'Who do you say I am?'

RECALL THE STORY: 'DIDN'T YOU KNOW?'

- Why were Kaylum and Ryan staying at their Nana's house?
- What was the first picture they saw in Nana's photo album? Why did it surprise them?
- What else did they discover about Nana from looking at the photos?

JESUS, THE PROMISED MESSIAH

The prophet Isaiah in the Old Testament promised that, when the time was right, God would send a gentle and loving servant to be the people's leader. This person would be their Saviour, their **Messiah**. Centuries later, Jesus stood up in his local synagogue in Nazareth and read out Isaiah's message about the promised Messiah. He told the people that he himself was that Messiah. Now read the story as it is told in the Gospel according to Luke.

Jesus Is the Messiah (Luke 4:16-22)

Then Jesus went to Nazareth, where he had been brought up, and on the Sabbath he went as usual to the synagogue. He stood up to read the Scriptures and was handed the book of the prophet Isaiah. He unrolled the scroll and found the place where it is written,

'The Spirit of the Lord is upon me,
because he has chosen me to bring good news to the poor.
He has sent me to proclaim liberty to captives
and recovery of sight to the blind,
to set free the oppressed
and announce that the time has come
when the Lord will save his people.'

Jesus rolled up the scroll, gave it back to the attendant, and sat down. All the people in the synagogue had their eyes fixed on him, as he said to them, 'This passage of scripture has come true today, as you heard it being read.'

They were all impressed with him and marvelled at the eloquent words that he spoke. They said, 'Isn't he the son of Joseph?'

- In what town was the synagogue that Jesus went to on the Sabbath?
- What book did Jesus read from?
- Name some of the people who were mentioned in the Scripture passage that Jesus read out.

JOURNAL EXERCISE

- Record some of the things the promised Messiah would do, according to the passage from the Book of Isaiah that Jesus read out in the synagogue.

A QUESTION FOR ALL CHRISTIANS

One day, when Jesus was walking near Caesarea Philippi with his disciples, he asked his disciples a question. Here is the story as it is told in the Gospel according to Mark:

'Who do you say I am?' (Mark 8:27-29)

Jesus and his disciples went away to the villages round Caesarea Philippi. On the way he asked them, 'Tell me, who do people say I am?'

'Some say that you are John the Baptist,' they answered; 'others say that you are Elijah, while others say that you are one of the prophets.'

'What about you?' he asked them. 'Who do you say I am?'

Peter answered, 'You are the Messiah.'

FOR MEMORISATION

'You are the Messiah.' (Mark 8:29)

- What was the first question that Jesus asked his disciples while they were walking together?
- What people did the disciples mention in their answer?
- What was the second question that Jesus asked them?

JOURNAL EXERCISE

- Imagine Jesus asks you the question, 'Who do you say I am?' What answer would you give? Write your answer in your Religious Education journal.

AT HOME

DID YOU KNOW?

Jesus is the Messiah, the Christ, the Saviour whom God promised through the prophets.

THIS WEEK

The children heard how, as the apostles got to know Jesus, they began to realise that, not only was he a teacher, a healer and a miracle worker, he was actually the Messiah, the Christ, the Saviour whom God had promised through the prophets. The apostles knew this because they made connections between what the prophets said and what happened in the life of Jesus. When Jesus finally asked the apostles the question, 'Who do you say I am?', Peter answered, 'You are the Messiah.'

Pray this prayer together:

Lord Jesus,
You are the Messiah whom God promised.
You came to show us how to live and how to love.
Help us to learn about you, and to learn from you.
Help us to live as you taught us. Amen.

TIME TOGETHER

Chat Together
Chat about how you get to know people better when you spend time with them. Think of someone whom you have come to know better this year. Talk about how your family could get to know Jesus better; for example, by praying to him and by reading stories about him from the Bible.

Record and Share
Who in your own family are you especially close to? What things do you do to stay close to each other? Write about the person and the things you do together in your Religious Education journal. Then share your work with that person.

Be Open
Be open to learning more about Jesus and to saying 'Yes' to confirming your belief in him.

THIS WEEK IN SCHOOL

You are invited to think about:
- How God calls each one of us
- Stories from the Bible in which God called people to undertake particular tasks
- What your Christian vocation may be

KEY WORD

Christian Vocation: A unique call from God to each one of us, inviting us to love and serve him and his Church by living as Jesus asks us to.

THEME 3: OUR CHRISTIAN VOCATION | LESSON 1

God Calls Each One of Us

RECALL THE STORY: 'THE SCHOOL REUNION'

- What anniversary was Scoil Bríd celebrating?
- How was the school marking this special occasion?
- When did Oran's love of building begin?
- Why was no one surprised to hear that Carmel was a vet?
- Why did Jean enjoy her work at the day centre?
- What motivated Tim to be a homemaker?
- What experience early in his life made Rian realise that he wanted to be a nurse?
- Why was no one surprised to hear that Caoimhe was involved in music and acting?
- Why had Naoise chosen to switch career and become a social worker?

THINK ABOUT IT ...

- What do you think you would like to be when you grow up? What abilities and talents do you have that might help you to do that job well?

OUR CHRISTIAN VOCATION

As Christians we believe that God calls and draws each one of us to a certain way of living. This is known as a **Christian vocation** or a calling. The word 'vocation' comes from the Latin word *vocare*, which means 'to call'. God invites us to love and serve him and his Church through whatever way we choose to live our life. Jesus has provided a model for us of how to live in love of God and of others.

GOD CALLED SAMUEL

You have heard the stories from the Old Testament about God calling Abraham, Moses and Jeremiah. Here is another story from the Old Testament. It is about God calling a boy named Samuel. After receiving guidance from a man named Eli about how to be a servant of the Lord, Samuel answered God's call.

The Lord Appears to Samuel (1 Samuel 3:2-10)

One night Eli, who was now almost blind, was sleeping in his own room; Samuel was sleeping in the sanctuary, where the sacred Covenant Box was. Before dawn, while the lamp was still burning, the Lord called Samuel. He answered, 'Yes, sir!' and ran to Eli and said, 'You called me, and here I am.'

But Eli answered, 'I didn't call you; go back to bed.' So Samuel went back to bed.

The Lord called Samuel again. The boy did not know that it was the Lord, because the Lord had never spoken to him before. So he got up, went to Eli, and said, 'You called me, and here I am.'

But Eli answered, 'My son, I didn't call you; go back to bed.'

The Lord called Samuel a third time; he got up, went to Eli, and said, 'You called me, and here I am.'

Then Eli realised that it was the Lord who was calling the boy, so he said to him, 'Go back to bed; and if he calls you again, say, "Speak, Lord, your servant is listening."' So Samuel went back to bed.

The Lord came and stood there, and called as he had before, 'Samuel! Samuel!'

Samuel answered, 'Speak; your servant is listening.'

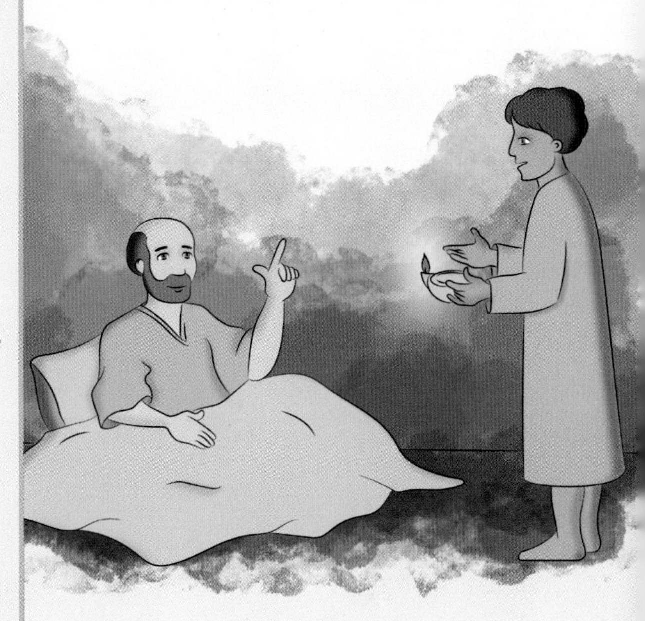

- Who did Samuel think was calling him?
- How did he respond each time he heard the call?
- How many times did Samuel hear the call before Eli realised it was from the Lord?
- What did Eli tell Samuel to do if he heard the call again?
- How did Samuel respond when he realised that it was the Lord who was calling him?

The Bible tells us that Samuel went on to become a judge and a prophet. He was also a leader of the people of Israel. He never stopped listening and responding to God's call.

LOOK AND RESPOND

The New Testament also contains stories about people who were called. Can you name each of the people who are being called in these pictures? Look up the Scripture references to read their stories.

Luke 1:28-38

Matthew 4:18-20

Matthew 4:21-22

Luke 5:27-28

Luke 19:1-6

FOR MEMORISATION

A Christian vocation is a unique call from God to each one of us, inviting us to love and serve him and his Church by living as Jesus asks us to.

JOURNAL EXERCISE

- Choose one of the people from the pictures and pretend you are that person. Write the diary entry that you might have written on the day that you were called.

GOD CALLS US

We know that God doesn't call us today in the same way that he called people back in biblical times. Sometimes, God's call is that little voice inside us that prompts us to do what is right. God's call to us to love and serve others and to do what is right is our vocation as followers of Jesus.

THIS WEEK

The children learned that a Christian vocation is a unique call from God to each one of us, inviting us to love and serve him and his Church by living as Jesus asks us to. There are lots of stories about people being called in the Bible. This week the children heard the story from the Old Testament of God calling a boy named Samuel to be his prophet. The children also recalled how God called Mary, through the angel Gabriel, to be the mother of Jesus, and how Jesus called the disciples Peter, Andrew, James and John. God calls each of us too. God is waiting for us to respond to his call, just as Samuel did when he said, 'Speak; your servant is listening.'

Read the poem 'The Call' together.

The Call

I wondered what path my life should take;
Would I marry, be single, which choice would I make?
Would I play football or sing like a star?
Run my own business and go really far?

Having no idea where I should start,
I felt God whisper deep in my heart,
'Dear child, my plans for you are great.'
I became anxious, 'O Lord, please wait!'

'Come, follow me,' God seemed to say,
'I will guide you each step of the way.
A special path I have chosen for you;
While tough at times, it will always be true.'

'It's not just about the job that you do;
It's who you are. Are you honest and true?'
'What is this path, dear God above?'
'It's simple,' God smiled, 'it's the path of love.'

AT HOME

DID YOU KNOW?

God calls each of us to live a life of love.

TIME TOGETHER

Respond and Share

Think about a time when you sensed that God was calling you to do an act of kindness. Write about it in your Religious Education journal. Then share what you have written with your parent or guardian.

Pray Together

Lord, we believe you call each one of us.
You call us to live in the way Jesus showed us – by loving you and our neighbour.
Help us to see, hear and feel the ways in which you draw us to you, to others and to our true selves.
We ask this through Christ our Lord. Amen.

Be Ready

Many of the people whom God called in biblical times were confused at first. They weren't sure that God was calling them. Be ready to listen to the voice of God in your own heart, calling and encouraging you to lead a life of love.

THIS WEEK IN SCHOOL

You are invited to think about:

- The different ways in which people respond to God's call
- The opportunities we have in our daily lives to respond to God's call
- How you can respond to God's call

KEY WORD

Venerable: An official title given by the Church to a deceased person who, through his/her life, has reached a degree of holiness but who has not yet been made a saint.

THEME 3: OUR CHRISTIAN VOCATION | LESSON 2

We Respond to God's Call

PEOPLE RESPOND TO GOD'S CALL

God calls every person to a specific vocation – to live their life in such a way that they serve God and others. Throughout history, millions of people have been inspired by the life of Jesus to answer 'yes' to God's call. Some of these people were single and some of them were married; some were priests and some were sisters; some were men and some were women; some were old and some were young. These people who answered God's call came from many different countries, had different skin colours, and spoke many different languages. But they all had one thing in common: they all saw things that needed to be done in order to make the Kingdom of God that Jesus spoke about a reality in our world. All of these people responded to God's call to help bring about such a world by loving others as Jesus did.

HOW MIGHT YOU RESPOND?

Read the following descriptions of the kind of situations that happen in everyday life that offer people an opportunity to respond to God's call to love and serve others.

There is a collection outside your local shop for the St Vincent de Paul society. They are raising money to help people who are homeless. You just got some money from your uncle for your birthday.

- What might God be calling you to do?
- How might you respond?

You and some of your friends are part of a group on social media. One of your friends has started to make fun of a boy in your class, commenting in a mean and nasty way about the way he looks.

- What might God be calling you to do?
- How might you respond?

Your teacher is looking for someone to be a 'buddy' to one of the younger children in the yard who has no one to play with them.

- What might God be calling you to do?
- How might you respond?

THINK ABOUT IT ...

- Look back at the three scenarios. Think about the kind of person you need to be in order to respond as God desires in such situations. Think about how you can try harder to be that kind of person.

JOURNAL EXERCISE

- Work on your own or with a friend. In your Religious Education journal make a list of people whom you think have responded well to God's call. Write about some of the things these people have done or are doing so as to live in the way Jesus showed us and help to build up the Body of Christ in the world.

Learn by Example: Nano Nagle

Nano Nagle was born in 1718 in Ballygriffin in County Cork. At that time in Ireland there were laws, known as the Penal Laws, which denied Catholics the right to education and the right to own property. Because Nano's parents were wealthy, she and her siblings were educated at home and in the local hedge school. At the age of ten Nano was sent to a Benedictine convent in Flanders in France to continue her education. At sixteen she went to Paris to study there.

In Paris Nano lived with relatives and had a wonderful life mixing with wealthy people and attending parties and dances. One night, on the way home from a dance, she noticed some poor people waiting outside a church looking for food and shelter. Nano realised how difficult their lives were in comparison to her own, and she came to see that her vocation was to help the poor.

When Nano returned to Ireland, she and her sister Ann began visiting and helping poor families. Shortly afterwards Ann died.

Nano thought the best way for her to help the poor was to become a nun, and so she joined a convent in Paris. She found she didn't have enough opportunities to help the poor there, so she returned to live with her brother and his wife in Cork. Nano decided to begin educating the poor girls of the area, so she set up a school in Cove Lane, now Douglas Street, in Cork, which was attended by thirty-five girls. Soon she had schools in other parts of Cork city.

Nano could have been arrested for educating Catholics, so she had to work in secret. Within ten years she was operating ten schools, teaching both boys and girls. She used to get up at four a.m. each day and go around all the schools supporting the children and teachers, and by night she visited the poor of Cork city. She carried a lantern (lamp) at night, which earned her the name 'The Lady of the Lantern'.

The Sisters of the Presentation, the religious order that Nano founded on Christmas Eve 1775, has convents and schools all over the world today, and countless children have been educated because of Nano's spirit and determination to live a life of love by serving God and others as Jesus asked.

Nano died of tuberculosis on 26 April 1784. Her last message to her sisters was 'Love one another as you have hitherto done'. Pope Francis gave Nano the title '**Venerable** Nano' in 2013, which is an honour the Pope gives as the second of four stages in becoming a saint.

FOR MEMORISATION

Give thanks to the Lord,
because he is good,
and his love is eternal.
(Psalms 118:1)

- What kind of upbringing did Nano have? Was her family wealthy or poor?
- What happened in Paris that caused Nano to decide to work on behalf of those who were less well off than herself?
- Where did Nano start her first school for the education of poor children?
- Why was Nano called 'The Lady of the Lantern'?
- What religious order was founded by Nano in 1775?

AT HOME

THIS WEEK

The children explored further the concept of Christian vocation, and the different ways people can live out their vocation, whether they are single or married, in religious life or in ordained ministry. The children looked at the example of Nano Nagle, whose selfless care for others changed the lives of children all over Ireland and, indeed, the world. Above all, they learned that they, too, can respond to God's call to love and serve him and others at this time in their lives by the way they treat the people whom they meet and interact with from day to day.

Chat about it ...

Think of people you know in your neighbourhood, such as a local shopkeeper, a school warden, a nurse, a teacher, a parent, a student in secondary school, someone who works in a garage. Chat together about different ways in which each of these people can live their Christian vocation.

DID YOU KNOW?

We can respond to God's call to love and serve him and others in our daily lives. We can do that no matter how young or how old we are, no matter where we live or where we come from. Nothing can stop us from living our vocation right here, right now.

TIME TOGETHER

Respond and Share

In your Religious Education journal, write about one thing that you and your family do to live out your vocation as followers of Jesus. Then share what you have written with your parent or guardian.

Pray Together

Pray the *Glory be to the Father* together.

Be Responsive

It's not always easy to act, even when you know what you *should* do. Pray for the courage to respond to God's call, even in difficult circumstances.

THIS WEEK IN SCHOOL

You are invited to think about:

- Your hopes and dreams
- The hopes and dreams of the people of Israel as they waited for the Messiah
- Zechariah and Elizabeth, and how their dreams to have a child came true
- The season of Advent as a time when we prepare to celebrate the coming or birth of Jesus at Christmas

KEY WORDS

Temple: Jewish place of worship.

Advent: The first season in the Liturgical Year. The word 'Advent' means 'coming'. The season of Advent marks the countdown of four weeks leading to the coming or birth of Jesus Christ.

THEME 4: ADVENT AND CHRISTMAS | LESSON 1

Zechariah Waits

HOPES AND DREAMS

We all have hopes and dreams for ourselves, for our families and even for the world.

JOURNAL EXERCISE

- What are your own hopes and dreams? Record them in your Religious Education journal using words, symbols and/or drawings.

THE HOPES AND DREAMS OF THE JEWISH PEOPLE

The hopes and dreams of the Israelites centred on the coming of the Messiah, whom God had promised through the prophets. These hopes lived on in the Jewish people down through the centuries, right up to the time of Jesus. Some expected the Messiah to be a great king like David. Some thought that the Messiah would be a freedom fighter who would end Roman rule and free Israel.

RECALL THE STORY: 'GOD SENDS THE ANGEL GABRIEL TO ZECHARIAH'

Elizabeth and Zechariah lived in hope of seeing the Messiah. They also dreamed of having a child of their own.

- What kind of people were Elizabeth and Zechariah? Were they religious?
- What was Zechariah's job?
- What message did the angel Gabriel bring to Zechariah? What did the angel say about the son that Zechariah and Elizabeth would have?
- How did Zechariah respond to the angel's message?
- What happened to Zechariah because he found it so difficult to believe the angel's message?
- How did the people standing outside know that Zechariah had a vision while he was in the **Temple**?

THINK ABOUT IT ...

- If you were told that your prayer was going to be answered, even though it seemed impossible, how would you feel or react? What might you do while you were waiting for your prayer to be answered?

THE BIRTH OF JOHN THE BAPTIST

This is the story of the birth of John the Baptist as it is told in the Gospel according to Luke.

The Birth of John the Baptist (Luke 1:57-66)

The time came for Elizabeth to have her baby, and she gave birth to a son. Her neighbours and relatives heard how wonderfully good the Lord had been to her, and they all rejoiced with her.

When the baby was a week old, ... they were going to name him Zechariah, after his father. But his mother said, 'No! His name is to be John.'

They said to her, 'But you don't have any relative with that name!' Then they made signs to his father, asking him what name he would like the boy to have.

Zechariah asked for a writing pad and wrote, 'His name is John.' How surprised they all were! At that moment, Zechariah was able to speak again, and he started praising God. The neighbours were all filled with fear, and the news about these things spread through all the hill country of Judea. Everyone who heard of it thought about it and asked, 'What is this child going to be?' For it was plain that the Lord's power was upon him.

- What name did Elizabeth say the baby was to be called? Why was that?
- Why did their neighbours think that was not a good choice?
- How did Zechariah communicate what he thought the baby should be called?
- What amazing thing happened then to Zechariah?

The Naming of John the Baptist
by Fra Angelico (c. 1430)

This painting shows Zechariah and Elizabeth bringing their child to the Temple when he was ten days old. This was something that all religious Jews would have been expected to do.

JOURNAL EXERCISE

- In the time of Jesus, Jewish children were given their names because of their meaning and not because of how they sounded. In your journal, write and decorate your own name, and write anything you know about why you were given that name. Then research the meaning of your name, and write down what you discover.

ADVENT: OUR TIME OF WAITING

Advent is a special time in the Church calendar. It marks the beginning of the Liturgical (Church) Year and the four-week countdown to the feast of the Nativity, 25 December, when we remember and celebrate the birth of Jesus. Advent is the time when we prepare for and look forward to reliving this great event. It is a time of prayer and hope, as we wait to welcome Christ once again into our hearts and into our lives. During Advent we remember, too, how Mary waited for the birth of her Son, Jesus, and how Elizabeth and Zechariah also waited for God's plan to unfold.

JOURNAL EXERCISE

During Advent we watch, wait and wonder. What are you watching for, waiting for and wondering about during this Advent season? Complete these sentences in your Religious Education journal:

- During Advent I will **watch** for ...
- During Advent I will **wait** for ...
- During Advent I will **wonder** about ...

FOR MEMORISATION

O my God,
I put my hope in you
because I am sure of your
promises.

THIS WEEK

The children recalled how the people of Ancient Israel waited for the coming of the Messiah – whom God had promised through the prophets. The prophets told the people about the Messiah, but nobody knew when he would come. And so the people watched and waited and wondered. The children also recalled that Zechariah was an old man when the angel Gabriel came to him to tell him the good news that his wife, Elizabeth, would have a child, and that the child, John, would prepare the way for the Messiah. The children heard once again the story of the birth of John the Baptist, and how John came to have that name. In this season of Advent, Christians wait to remember and celebrate the birth of Jesus, the Messiah and Saviour.

Read the poem 'Patient People' together.

Patient People

Advent is like a waiting room
for those who take time to make
an appointment with the Spirit of Christmas,
the real one, that is, not the fake
that's everywhere available, twenty-four seven
and in jingling tills rejoices;
the one you plug-in and it squawks 'Merry Christmas'
in battery-operated voices;
the one whose lights get brighter and brasher
with every year that goes by,
as they try to outdo each other:
they'll never outshine that star in the sky.

Those who have made an appointment
with the true spirit of Christmas know
that waiting rooms are unpopular places
in today's world of get-up-and-go.
What can you do in a waiting room but wait
and wait ... till the time is right
and the door to Christmas swings open
and patient people gain insight
to the Christian meaning of Christmas
which sings out in true festive voice,
'Come! Your waiting is over!
Emmanuel! God with us! Rejoice!'

AT HOME

DID YOU KNOW?

Mary, the mother of Jesus, and Elizabeth, Zechariah's wife, were cousins. Mary visited Elizabeth when both of them were pregnant.

TIME TOGETHER

Chat Together
Reflect together about the hopes and dreams that you have for your family, rather than just for yourself. Think about your extended family as well as your immediate family.

Respond and Share
Write about some of the hopes and dreams you have for your family. Share what you have written with your parent or guardian.

Be Hopeful
Advent is a time of waiting and a time of hope. During Advent we often see signs of hope in the world, such as people being a little more cheerful, a little more charitable or a little more thoughtful. Think about how you, too, can be a sign of hope.

THIS WEEK IN SCHOOL

You are invited to think about:

- Advent as a time of waiting
- How St Joseph waited for the birth of Jesus
- The role of St Joseph in the Christmas story

KEY WORDS

Genealogy: The study of ancestry – the line of descent of a person, family or group from an ancestor. The genealogy of Jesus is given at the start of Matthew's Gospel.

Ministry: Work. Jesus' ministry refers to the work God the Father sent him to do on earth. In the Church, ministry refers to work that is done in service of others.

THEME 4: ADVENT AND CHRISTMAS | LESSON 2

Joseph Waits

RECALL THE STORY: 'I CAN'T WAIT!'

- What did Jenny wish for when she stirred the cake mixture?
- What did Jenny, her mam and Shane use to make the Advent wreath? What do the candles on the Advent wreath represent?
- Why did their mam like to send Christmas cards? What kind of Christmas cards did she choose?
- On what day did they get the Christmas tree?
- Why did they not place the baby Jesus in the crib along with the other figures?
- What great news did they get when they arrived home from the carol service?

JOURNAL EXERCISE

- How does your family prepare for Christmas during Advent? Draw a picture and write a paragraph about it in your Religious Education journal.

ST JOSEPH, FOSTER FATHER OF JESUS

There is very little written about St Joseph in the Bible. We know from his **genealogy** in the Gospel according to Matthew that he was a descendant of King David, Israel's greatest king, and that he was born in Bethlehem, near Jerusalem. At some stage he moved to Nazareth in Galilee, where he worked as a carpenter. It was probably in Nazareth that Joseph became engaged (betrothed) to Mary. In Jewish culture, betrothal was considered the same as marriage in everything but name.

Joseph was a good man, who was faithful to God and to the Law, and God chose him to be the foster father of Jesus. St Joseph wasn't a rich man. When he took Jesus to the Temple for the first time, he offered the sacrifice of two turtledoves or a pair of pigeons – a sacrifice that was only allowed from those who couldn't afford to offer a lamb. It is believed that St Joseph died before Jesus began his **ministry**.

There are two feast days of St Joseph. The Feast of St Joseph the Husband of Mary is celebrated on 19 March, and it is the most commonly celebrated feast day for Joseph. In 1955 Pope Pius XII established the Feast of St Joseph the Worker, to be celebrated on 1 May. This is also May Day (International Workers' Day).

JOSEPH'S DREAM

The angel of the Lord first appeared to Joseph in a dream after Mary, to whom he was engaged, told him that she was pregnant by the power of the Holy Spirit. Now read the story as it is told in the Gospel according to Matthew.

Joseph's Dream (Matthew 1:18-24)

Mary was engaged to Joseph, but before they were married, she found out that she was going to have a baby by the power of the Holy Spirit. Joseph was a man who always did what was right, but he did not want to disgrace Mary publicly; so he made plans to break the engagement privately. While he was thinking about this, an angel of the Lord appeared to him in a dream and said, 'Joseph, descendant of David, do not be afraid to take Mary to be your wife. For it is by the Holy Spirit that she has conceived. She will have a son, and you will name him Jesus – because he will save his people from their sins.'

Now all this happened in order to make come true what the Lord had said through the prophet, 'A virgin will become pregnant and have a son, and he will be called Immanuel' (which means 'God is with us').

So when Joseph woke up, he married Mary, as the angel of the Lord had told him to.

- How did Joseph feel when he heard that Mary was pregnant?
- What did he think he might do? Why was he considering that?
- What happened to put his mind at rest?
- What name did the angel say Joseph and Mary should give the baby?
- What does the name 'Immanuel' mean?

ROLE-PLAY ACTIVITY

- With a partner, prepare and act out a conversation Joseph might have had with one of his friends after the angel appeared to him in his dream.

THE CHRISTMAS STORY

These pictures will help you to recall the Christmas story, beginning with the Annunciation and ending with the Holy Family's escape into Egypt.

FOR MEMORISATION

Come, let us praise the Lord!
Let us sing for joy to God,
who protects us!
(Psalms 95:1)

JOURNAL EXERCISE

- Record your favourite elements from the Christmas story in your Religious Education journal, using words and/or images.

AT HOME

THIS WEEK

The children explored St Joseph's role in the Christmas story. God chose Joseph to be the foster father of Jesus and the husband of Mary. Joseph was loving and supportive of Mary in her role as mother of Jesus. As we wait for Christmas, we remember that St Joseph also waited to welcome Jesus into the world.

Pray this prayer together:

St Joseph,
God chose you to be the husband of Mary and the foster father of Jesus.
You protected and loved the Holy Family.
Pray for us and our family. Amen.

Saint Joseph
by Guido Reni (c. 1605)

DID YOU KNOW?

There are two feast days of St Joseph: the Feast of St Joseph the Husband of Mary on 19 March, and the Feast of St Joseph the Worker on 1 May.

TIME TOGETHER

Chat Together
Reflect on the role St Joseph played as a foster father to Jesus and husband to Mary. Talk about what makes a good father, stepfather, foster father, godfather or grandfather.

Respond and Share
Think of a person you know who loves and protects their family. That is what St Joseph did. Write about that person in your Religious Education journal. Then share what you have written with your parent or guardian.

Be Loving
Joseph was a caring husband and a loving father. As you move closer to Christmas, consider what role everyone in your family can play, in the spirit of St Joseph, to make your home a peaceful and loving place.

THIS WEEK IN SCHOOL

You are invited to think about:

- How Christians are part of a worldwide family
- How Christmas is celebrated in different parts of the world
- The differences between the commercial and the religious celebration of Christmas

KEY WORDS

Global: Relating to the whole world.

Secular: Word used to describe things that are not religious, or not associated with religion.

THEME 4: ADVENT AND CHRISTMAS | LESSON 3

Christians Celebrate the Birth of Jesus

CELEBRATIONS

Celebrations are an important part of the life of every person and every family. Each year we celebrate lots of different occasions in our family, with our friends, as a country, and even as a **global** community.

JOURNAL EXERCISE

- Make a list of all the things you can think of that are celebrated each month of the year. They may be things you celebrate personally or things that you know are celebrated by other people. Then underline the ones that you and your family celebrate.

CELEBRATING CHRISTMAS

Christians are the largest religious group in the world. There are over two billion Christians living on planet Earth. Depending on where they live and their background, Christians may celebrate Christmas in very different ways. Even those Christians who live in Ireland can have different Christmas traditions. Let's see how two children whose families came to Ireland from another country celebrate Christmas.

Wiktoria, whose family is from Poland:

'Our big Christmas celebration is on Christmas Eve, rather than Christmas Day. In the evening time, Polish friends come over to our home and we have a big supper together. After we eat, we put up the Christmas tree. Yes, we don't do it until then! Even though we live in Ireland, we like keeping our Polish customs. The last thing we do on Christmas Eve is go to Mass.'

Carp is the chief dish served during *Wigilia*, the traditional Polish meal on Christmas Eve

Kojo, whose family is from Egypt:
'Our family is not Catholic – we are Coptic Christians. In Egypt, where my father comes from, Christmas is celebrated on 7 January rather than 25 December. Because my mum is Irish, we are allowed to celebrate Christmas twice! On 25 December we do the usual Irish stuff, and on 7 January we do the Egyptian stuff. One of the best things about 25 December is that we get to break our Advent fast. For forty-three days before Christmas, from 25 November to 6 January, we Coptics have a special fast where we don't eat anything that comes from animals. It's not easy, especially because we live in Ireland and there's loads of chocolate and other treats around at that time of year! Still, it's nice to be able to celebrate Christmas twice!'

SECULAR CELEBRATIONS OF CHRISTMAS

Some of our Christmas celebrations have to do with celebrating the birth of Jesus; for example, going to Mass and having a crib in our home. Other customs, while originally linked to Christian meaning, often have very little to do with Jesus, such as buying big presents for people, decorating our homes with Christmas trees and other items, using non-religious Advent calendars, and so on.

Some people who are not Christian still like to celebrate the non-religious, or **secular**, aspects of Christmas. Some people who are Christian celebrate both the religious and the non-religious aspects of Christmas. Other Christians try to make sure that their Christmas celebrations are all about celebrating Jesus' birthday, and nothing else.

THINK ABOUT IT ...

- Do you think it is important for Christians to celebrate the religious aspect of Christmas? Why or why not?

AN IRISH CHRISTMAS TRADITION

It is an old Irish Christmas tradition to place a lighted candle in windows on Christmas Eve as a sign of hospitality and welcome. It is also a reminder of how Mary and Joseph sought shelter and a warm place where Mary could have her baby. A lighted candle is, therefore, a Christmas decoration that has both a religious and a non-religious meaning.

FOR MEMORISATION

Research and learn how to say 'Happy Christmas' in three languages other than English.

CHRISTMAS AROUND THE WORLD

People all over the world celebrate Christmas in different ways.

In **Poland** people often celebrate a special supper called *Wigilia* on Christmas Eve.

Children in **Australia** celebrate Christmas during their summer holidays.

In **Hungary** children receive a visit from 'Mikulas' or St Nicholas.

In **Mexico** a special celebration called *La Posada* takes place between 16 December and Christmas Eve.

In Caracas, the capital of **Venezuela**, there's a tradition of people roller-skating to Mass from 16 to 24 December.

Most Catholics in **Brazil** go to Midnight Mass on Christmas Eve, after which there are often big firework displays.

JOURNAL EXERCISE

- Record in your Religious Education journal some of the ways you celebrate the religious meaning of Christmas. Use words and/or images.

THIS WEEK

The children explored how Christmas is celebrated in different ways by different people all over the world. We all have our own Christmas traditions. But, no matter what traditions we observe, all Christians should remember that Christmas is about celebrating the birth of Jesus. For this reason, we should try to keep religious traditions alive in our homes.

Read together the following passage from the book of the prophet Isaiah. It is one of the Scripture readings at the Vigil Mass on Christmas Eve.

Isaiah 9:2-3, 6

The people who walked in darkness
have seen a great light.
They lived in a land of shadows,
but now light is shining on them.
You have given them great joy, Lord;
you have made them happy.

A child is born to us!
A son is given to us!
And he will be our ruler.
He will be called, 'Wonderful Counsellor',
'Mighty God', 'Eternal Father',
'Prince of Peace'.

AT HOME

DID YOU KNOW?

Jesus is the 'reason for the season'. Christmas is about remembering and celebrating the birth of Jesus.

TIME TOGETHER

Chat Together

Talk about your own family's Christmas traditions and customs. Perhaps there are some more religious customs you could introduce this year.

Respond and Share

Write a paragraph about how your family celebrates Christmas Eve and/or Christmas Day. Share what you have written with your parent or guardian.

Pray Together

Loving God, may we have a safe, happy and healthy Christmas with our loved ones. Bless all those who visit our home this Christmas, and bless those whose homes we visit. Amen.

Be Mindful

Remember that Jesus is the 'reason for the season'. Try to keep Jesus at the centre of your Christmas celebrations and to spread his love to all the people you meet.

THIS WEEK IN SCHOOL

You are invited to think about:

- How much God loves you
- How you can become the person God calls you to be
- How your conscience helps you to know right from wrong

KEY WORD

Conscience: The 'voice of God' within us that helps us to know whether something is right or wrong.

THEME 5: CONSCIENCE | LESSON 1

We Can Hear God's Voice Within Us

WHAT KIND OF PERSON ARE YOU?

Each one of us has different qualities. Some of these qualities are good, like our kindness and compassion towards others, or our honesty and faithfulness. Some of our qualities are not good, such as our tendency to be greedy or jealous or tell lies. Every day we express our different qualities in different ways with different people and in different situations. How we use and develop our different qualities helps to make us into the sort of person we are now and will become.

THINK ABOUT IT ...

- If someone asked you to describe yourself, what might you say? What words would you use to describe the sort of person you are?
- If someone else was asked to describe the sort of person you are, what might he/she say? Why do you think they would describe you that way? Would a friend say something different to what your parent/guardian or teacher might say?

A Tale of Two Seeds

One evening a grandfather told his grandson about a battle that goes on inside people. He said, 'My son, the battle is between two "seeds" inside us all. One seed wants to sprout anger, jealousy, greed, self-pity, guilt, lies, and the feeling of being better than everyone else. The other seed wants to sprout joy, peace, love, hope, serenity, kindness, generosity, truth, and faith.'

The grandson thought about this for a minute and then he asked his grandfather: 'Which seed wins?'

The grandfather replied, 'The one you feed.'

- What battle did the grandfather say goes on inside people?
- What words did the grandfather use to describe what sprouts from the two seeds?
- What question did the grandson ask at the end of the story?
- What was the grandfather's answer?

THINK ABOUT IT ...

- In the story, the grandfather talked about a battle inside people between good things like joy, peace, love and hope, and bad things like jealousy, greed, lies and the feeling of being better than everyone else. Think about the good and bad feelings you have at different times, and about which of these feelings usually win out in the end.

BECOMING THE PERSON GOD CALLS YOU TO BE

We become the best person we can be, the person God calls us to be, by practising being that kind of person – choosing to do good things rather than bad things, choosing to do what is right instead of what is wrong. This practice takes time and patience, courage and determination.

Jesus showed us what is good. God has also given us a **conscience**, which is the voice of God inside us that prompts us to do what is right.

JOURNAL EXERCISE

- In your Religious Education journal, use words and/or drawings to record some of the good things that your conscience prompts you to do in your day-to-day life.

Read this story from the Gospel of Matthew about a rich young man who came to Jesus because he was troubled.

Jesus and the Rich Young Man (Matthew 19:16-17, 20-22)

Once a man came to Jesus. 'Teacher,' he asked, 'what good thing must I do to receive eternal life?'

'Why do you ask me concerning what is good?' answered Jesus. 'There is only One who is good. Keep the commandments if you want to enter life.' ...

'I have obeyed all these commandments,' the young man replied. 'What else do I need to do?'

Jesus said to him, 'If you want to be perfect, go and sell all you have and give the money to the poor, and you will have riches in heaven; then come and follow me.'

When the young man heard this, he went away sad, because he was very rich.'

- What did the young man ask Jesus?
- What answer did Jesus give him?
- What did the young man do then?

FOR MEMORISATION

Our conscience is a gift from God. It helps us to know what is right and what is wrong so that we can make good choices.

AT HOME

DID YOU KNOW?

The way you act, and how you use your gifts and talents, shapes the sort of person you become.

THIS WEEK

The children learned that God wants us to become the best people we can possibly be, and by so doing reflect the goodness that is in each one of us. Our conscience is 'the voice of God' that speaks to us from our heart, guiding us to know right from wrong and to make good decisions. God gives us the freedom to follow our conscience. We can ask God to help us to become the people God wants us to be.

Read the poem 'The Voice Within' together.

The Voice Within

Each day we make decisions, some are big and some are small;
For some we may need help and for others none at all.
Some people like to choose for us and tell us what to do;
They may press us to do the things that they want us to.
Other people offer wisdom when we're struggling to decide;
They simply want the best for us, they're always on our side.

Despite the many voices that tend to come our way,
There's another voice to listen to each and every day;
It's the voice within that guides us and helps us to be strong;
From deep within it tells us what is right and what is wrong.
And even when we know the right thing that we should do,
It takes courage to go and do it, as other paths are tempting too.
So when faced with a decision and wanting to do what's best,
Just listen to the voice within and with wisdom you'll be blessed.

TIME TOGETHER

Chat Together

Talk about the kind of person you think you are, and the person you think you want to be.

Respond and Share

How can you 'feed' those things in you that are good, to make sure they grow so that you become the best person you can be? Write your answer in your Religious Education journal and share it with your parent or guardian.

Be Your Best Self

It is never too early to be the kind of person you want to be. Start practising today!

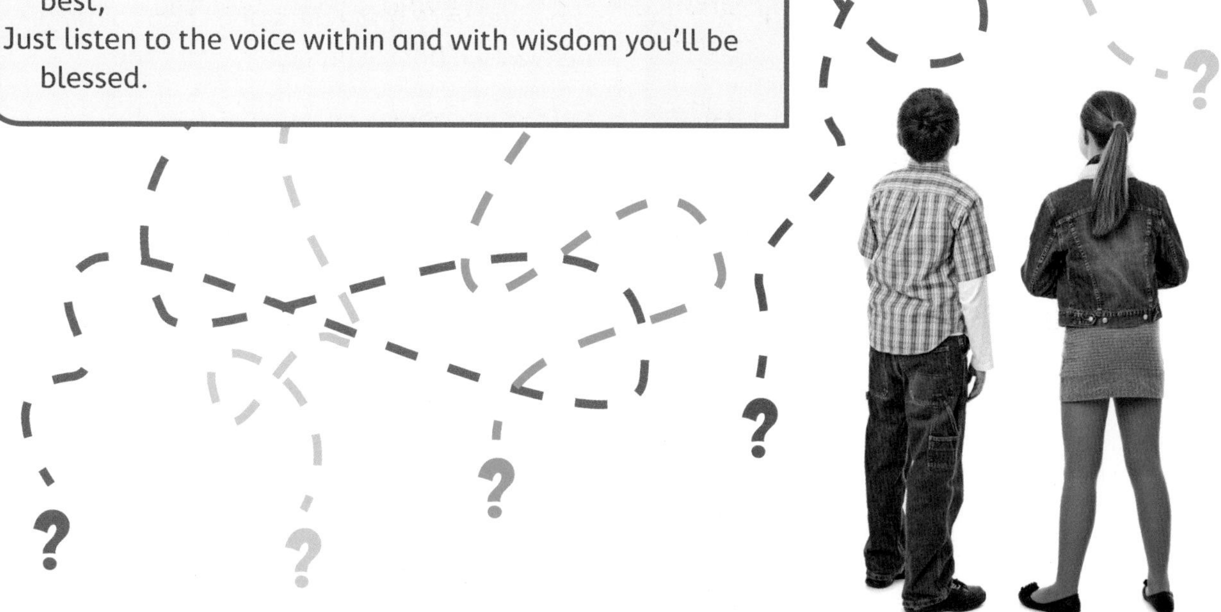

THIS WEEK IN SCHOOL

THIS WEEK IN SCHOOL

You are invited to think about:

- The people in your life who help you to recognise right from wrong
- How your conscience grows and develops over time
- All the things and people that help your conscience to grow

THEME 5: CONSCIENCE | LESSON 2

Our Conscience Develops As We Grow

RECALL THE STORY: 'JAMIE'S CONSCIENCE'

- Who was Con, and who gave him that name?
- Where could Con always be found?
- What kind of relationship did Jamie usually have with Con?
- What was happening recently that caused Con to be worried?
- Why wasn't Jamie able to hear Con's voice?
- What do you think Mr Rogers meant when he shouted at Jamie: 'Have you no conscience, boy?'
- How did things change when Jamie started to listen to Con again?

THINK ABOUT IT ...

- Do you always listen to your conscience, or are there times when, like Jamie, you ignore your conscience? What can happen when you stop listening to your conscience?

OUR CONSCIENCE GROWS AND DEVELOPS OVER TIME

Even very young children have a conscience, but we need to develop our conscience as we get older. We help our conscience to be better able to guide us about how to make good choices when we listen to the advice of the mature adults around us and to the teachings of the Church, when we learn about the things Jesus said and did, and when we listen to stories about people, such as the saints, who lived very good lives and tried to make the world a better place for everyone.

JOURNAL EXERCISE

- Think of a person who helps you learn what is right and what is wrong. Write about that person in your Religious Education journal.

LEARN BY EXAMPLE

Read this account of how Willie Bermingham came to establish the organisation called ALONE, which offers help and support to older people who are in need.

Willie Bermingham and ALONE

Willie Bermingham was born in Dublin in 1942. For many years he worked with Dublin Fire Brigade. He founded ALONE in 1977 following a winter when the Dublin Fire Brigade was called to retrieve the bodies of several older people who died unnoticed in appalling poverty. Willie was deeply disturbed by this and he felt himself called to do something to improve life for older people in Dublin. This is the story that Willie told about why he started ALONE.

> He was an old man in his seventies. He lived alone and he was very frail. He had sight in only one of his eyes and, like any man of his age, he tired easily.
>
> On a cold wet day in February, he left his little two-room timber chalet in a pensioners' settlement at Dublin's Charlemont Street. He returned later soaked right through and he was frozen. He was only able to take off his jacket. He lay on his bed and must have gained enough strength to pull some old blankets over him to keep warm. How long it took him to die, I don't know. I found him still clutching the blankets in his left hand and his right leg drawn up. The fire brigade had been called when someone noticed that they hadn't seen the old man out and about. No one could say how long it had been since they had seen him. I forced the window and climbed in, and, as I expected, there was another of a long list of what I had come to term 'my people' dead. His surroundings were small and cold. His presses were empty. Two empty coal bags lay beside the fire. There was nothing in the house that could have given the man any comfort at all. Like many old men and women, he had been cast away on the scrap heap. He was left to face loneliness, cold, hunger and depression behind the closed doors of a capital city. He had been sentenced to death, alone and in misery. It shocked me so much that I set up a society called ALONE.

ALONE still works to make people aware of the conditions faced by older people. It supports older people who have difficulties with loneliness, social isolation, poor health, poverty, poor housing or homelessness. It encourages people to visit and assist their neighbours who are older or living alone.

ALONE's slogan is: 'A Little Offering Never Ends.'

In response to the four-year campaign by ALONE for a task force to deal with the dire circumstances of older people, the Government allocated one million pounds to help the situation. As a result, a large number of older people were provided with basic facilities, including water, toilets and electricity. While this in no way solved all the problems, it did help ALONE considerably in their work.

Willie Bermingham died in 1990. His simple acts of kindness mean that his impact can still be felt today. ALONE continues to work for older people in Dublin and across the country and its volunteers continue to visit older people. Willie could never have imagined that ALONE would still be doing this work so many years after he started the organisation.

FOR MEMORISATION

The good choices we make in our lives every day can help to make the world we live in a better place.

THINK ABOUT IT ...

- What do you think of how Willie Bermingham tried to make the world a better place? How might the example of his life inspire you to try to make the world you live in a better place?

AT HOME

THIS WEEK

The children learned that their conscience develops as they grow, and that it is helped to develop by many different things, such as: the good example and advice they receive from the adults who guide and teach them; the words and actions of Jesus; what they learn at school, in church and from sacramental preparation; and the stories they hear about people who live good lives and try to make the world a better place. The children heard the story of Willie Bermingham, the founder of the ALONE organisation.

Pray this prayer together:

God our Father, thank you for the people who help us to recognise right from wrong.
Thank you for all those who show us how to live as Jesus asks us to.
Bless all these people and keep them safe.
Thank you for the gift of our conscience,
which has the power to transform our lives if we listen to it. Amen.

DID YOU KNOW?

No one is born with a fully formed conscience. Our conscience develops as we grow.

TIME TOGETHER

Chat Together
Talk about times when your conscience helped you to make the right choice in a difficult situation.

Respond and Share
In your Religious Education journal, write about a good choice you made that affected someone else's life, and what helped you to make that choice. Share what you have written with your parent or guardian.

Be Attentive
Try to remember, especially when you have to make a difficult choice, to listen to your conscience. It will help you to make the right choice.

THIS WEEK IN SCHOOL

You are invited to think about:

- How followers of Jesus are called to treat others with love and respect
- How Catholic social teaching can help us to be just and fair in our treatment of others
- How Jesus treated the Samaritan woman at the well with dignity and compassion

KEY WORDS

Migrant: A person who moves from one place to another to seek a better life.

Refugee: A person who has been forced to leave their country in order to escape war, persecution or a natural disaster.

THEME 6: SOCIAL JUSTICE | LESSON 1

Jesus Teaches Us to Act Justly

THE MIGRANT CRISIS AND THE IRISH NAVY'S RESPONSE

The 'European migrant crisis' refers to a period beginning in 2015 when large numbers of people arrived in Europe after travelling across the Mediterranean Sea or overland from Africa, Asia and the Middle East. This movement of people is still happening. Many of these people risk their lives trying to make their way to Europe in the hope of finding safety and peace and the chance to start a new life. Some flee their homes in search of a better life because of the poverty in their own country. These people are called **migrants**. Others are forced to leave their country in order to escape war, persecution or a natural disaster. These people are called **refugees**. Very often, these people sell everything they own in order to pay smugglers to get them into Europe. Often, the smugglers are only interested in the people's money and have no regard for their safely. They transport these desperate people across rough seas in poorly made boats that are overcrowded and not equipped for such purposes. Every year, many of these overcrowded boats sink, resulting in the deaths of thousands of men, women and children.

In response to this migrant crisis, the Irish Government asked men and women who serve in the Navy to go to the Mediterranean Sea and rescue as many people as they could. On board the Irish vessels, the migrants receive food, water and any medical treatment they need. Between May 2015 and June 2016, the Irish Navy rescued 15,621 people from the Mediterranean Sea.

THINK ABOUT IT ...

- Do you think the Irish Navy is right to help the migrants and refugees who are crossing the Mediterranean Sea? Why or why not?

A group of refugees and other migrants landing off the coast of Greece in 2015

MANY PEOPLE NEED TO BE RESCUED

It is very clear that migrants and refugees who find themselves in such desperate circumstances need to be rescued. But other people in very different situations also need to be rescued, even people who live in Ireland. Sometimes people end up in difficult situations because of unjust or unfair circumstances over which they have no control. For example, when a factory or other business closes down, the people who work there may no longer be able to afford to keep their home or feed their family. In Ireland in recent years, many people were left homeless because of the downturn in the economy. In some developing countries, people are starving because a lack of rainfall prevents them from growing crops with which to feed themselves and their families. People in such situations also need to be rescued.

JOURNAL EXERCISE

- Imagine you have to leave your home in a hurry to go to a place you do not know, and that you have been given just five minutes to pack. Draw a picture in your Religious Education journal to show how you are feeling.

Read this excerpt from the story of Jesus talking with the Samaritan woman at the well:

Jesus and the Woman at the Well (John 4:7-15)

A Samaritan woman came to draw some water, and Jesus said to her, 'Give me a drink of water.' (His disciples had gone into town to buy food.)

The woman answered, 'You are a Jew, and I am a Samaritan – so how can you ask me for a drink?' (Jews will not use the same cups and bowls that Samaritans use.)

Jesus answered, 'If you only knew what God gives and who it is that is asking you for a drink, you would ask him, and he would give you life-giving water.'

'Sir,' the woman said, 'you don't have a bucket, and the well is deep. Where would you get that life-giving water? It was our ancestor Jacob who gave us this well; he and his children and his flocks all drank from it. You don't claim to be greater than Jacob, do you?'

Jesus answered, 'Those who drink this water will get thirsty again, but those who drink the water that I will give them will never be thirsty again. The water that I will give them will become in them a spring which will provide them with life-giving water and give them eternal life.'

'Sir,' the woman said, 'give me that water! Then I will never be thirsty again, nor will I have to come here to draw water.'

FOR MEMORISATION

Jesus said, 'Those who drink the water that I will give them will never be thirsty again. The water that I will give them will become in them a spring which will provide them with life-giving water and give them eternal life.' (John 4:14)

THINK ABOUT IT ...

- What do you think Jesus meant when he spoke about 'life-giving water'?

KEY WORDS

Society: The larger community in which we live, as distinct from the smaller communities or neighbourhoods to which we belong.

Social justice: When a society is fair and just in its treatment of people, we say that social justice exists in that society.

Social teaching of the Catholic Church: The Catholic Church's teaching about acting with justice (fairness) towards other people.

Social injustice: When a society is unfair and unjust in its treatment of people, we say that there is social injustice in that society.

CHRISTIANS ARE CALLED TO WORK FOR SOCIAL JUSTICE

Jesus treated all people with respect, fairness and compassion. He reached out to those who were in need and he treated everyone as equals. In other words, he practised **social justice**.

The Church calls us to do the same. The **social teaching of the Catholic Church** provides us with guidelines for how we can work to change injustices that we see in our **society**, such as poverty, homelessness and the neglect or pollution of the environment. We respond to the invitation to work for social justice when we treat others fairly, when we share what we have with those in need, and when we support and stand up for people who are excluded or treated badly in our society.

There are many organisations working for social justice in Ireland and elsewhere. Christian Aid is an international aid agency that brings together members of different Christian Churches to work against inequality and injustice in society, both here in Ireland and overseas. The social justice charity Trócaire frequently works alongside Christian Aid to promote peace and justice as well as care of the environment throughout the world.

Our planet needs to be rescued and helped if it is to survive. Working to protect the natural world that is all around us and on which we all depend for our survival is also one of the ways in which we can work for social justice.

THIS WEEK

The children explored the concept of social justice and the Church's teaching that all people have the right to be treated with dignity and respect. They learned that all Christians are called to challenge injustices such as poverty and homelessness, to challenge systems that exclude or disadvantage people, and to work to put an end to actions that damage or destroy the environment. They looked at the examples of Trócaire and Christian Aid, both of which work to end injustices in society. The children also heard the story of Jesus speaking to the Samaritan woman at the well – a woman whom others had ignored and looked down upon.

Work together to complete the sentences in this reflection:

Life is an opportunity, benefit from it.
Life is beauty, admire it.
Life is a dream, realise it.
Life is a challenge, ________________.
Life is a promise, _________________.
Life is a song, _________________.
Life is precious, _________________.

AT HOME

DID YOU KNOW?

When we work for social justice, we are working to build the Kingdom of God on earth, as Jesus asked us to.

TIME TOGETHER

Chat Together

What **social injustice** would you most like to see an end to in our society? What could you do to work against this injustice, or to support those who suffer as a result of this injustice?

Pray Together

Help us, Lord, to build a world where everyone is treated equally and with dignity, as Jesus asked us to. Amen.

Be Just

Try always to be fair and just in your dealings with others, and to challenge situations of injustice wherever you see them.

THIS WEEK IN SCHOOL

You are invited to think about:

- How your attitude can affect the way you relate to other people
- How the Beatitudes can help you to be happy and bring happiness to others

KEY WORDS

Attitudes: People's thoughts and feelings about other people and things in the world around them.

Beatitudes: A set of good attitudes and values that Jesus urged his followers to put into practice in their lives.

Spiritually poor: People who are 'spiritually poor' know and are prepared to admit that they can be better people than they are. People who are 'spiritually poor' are also humble.

Humble: A humble person is someone who recognises that all of their talents and achievements are gifts from God. Humble people never boast about themselves or their achievements.

Persecute: To treat someone badly because of who they are or what they believe.

THEME 6: SOCIAL JUSTICE | LESSON 2

Jesus Teaches Us the Beatitudes

RECALL THE STORY: 'A BAD DAY FOR JOE!'

- How did Joe treat others in the story? What words would you use to describe his behaviour?
- Who did Joe affect by his actions? How did his actions affect these people?
- Did Joe always behave in this way, or was this behaviour unusual for him?

THINK ABOUT IT ...

- Do you sometimes feel as Joe did in the story? Why do you think that happens?

JOURNAL EXERCISE

- Draw an outline of yourself in your Religious Education journal. Add colours, symbols and/or words inside or around the outline to indicate what you are like when you are being your best self.

OUR ATTITUDES INFLUENCE OUR ACTIONS

Our **attitudes** are the thoughts and feelings we have about other people and things in the world around us. Our attitudes affect how we see other people and they influence our actions – the things we do. Attitudes can be positive or negative. Good attitudes usually lead to good actions, whereas bad attitudes tend to result in bad actions.

- In the story 'A Bad Day for Joe!', what was Joe's attitude to everything?
- What other attitudes – good and bad – can you name?

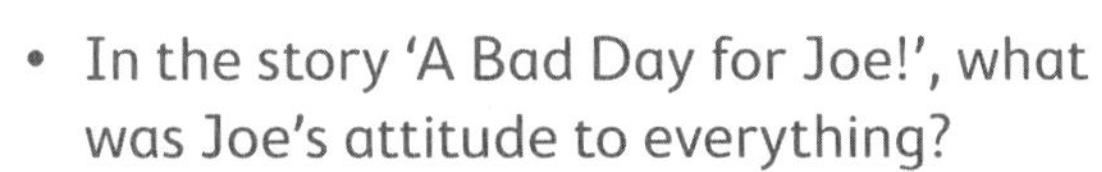

THE BEATITUDES

In the **Beatitudes**, Jesus presents us with a set of good attitudes and values that he wants us to put into practice in our lives. The word 'Beatitude' can be split into two words: 'be' and 'attitude'. The Beatitudes are 'good ways of being' in the world. Through his own words and actions, Jesus showed us how to live the Beatitudes. Jesus tells us that when we live by these attitudes, we will make ourselves and others happy.

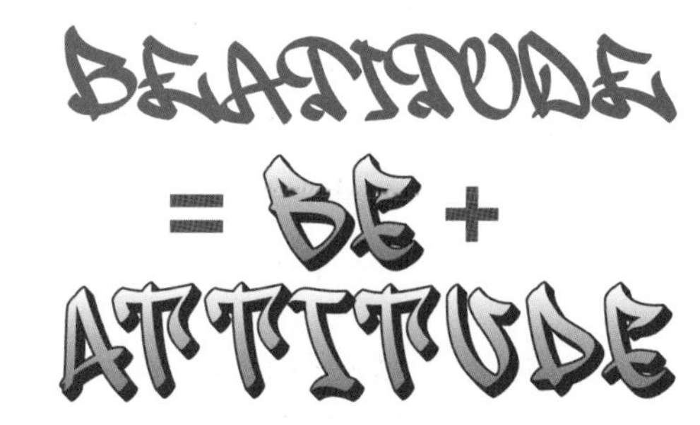

The Beatitudes are found in a passage known as the Sermon on the Mount in the Gospel according to Matthew.

The Beatitudes (Matthew 5:3-12)

Happy are those who know they are **spiritually poor**;
the Kingdom of heaven belongs to them!
Happy are those who mourn;
God will comfort them!
Happy are those who are **humble**;
they will receive what God has promised!
Happy are those whose greatest desire is to do what God requires;
God will satisfy them fully!
Happy are those who are merciful to others;
God will be merciful to them!
Happy are the pure in heart;
they will see God!
Happy are those who work for peace;
they will be called children of God!
Happy are those who are **persecuted** because they do what God requires;
the Kingdom of heaven belongs to them!
Happy are you when people insult you and persecute you and tell all kinds of evil lies against you because you are my followers. Be happy and glad, for a great reward is kept for you in heaven.

THINK ABOUT IT …

- What would the world be like if everyone lived by the attitudes that Jesus set out in the Beatitudes?
- What would the world be like if no one lived by these attitudes?

THE TEN COMMANDMENTS AND THE LAW OF LOVE

The Beatitudes are guidelines for how the followers of Jesus are to live their lives. But long before Jesus came on earth, God gave people another set of guidelines to help them live good lives. These guidelines were called the Ten Commandments. How many of the Ten Commandments can you remember?

Jesus also gave us a New Commandment. Unscramble the words below to read the key message in it:

eovl noe
hatoren

JOURNAL EXERCISE

- Record using words and/or images some of the ways in which people can live by the Beatitudes, the Ten Commandments and the New Commandment today.

FOR MEMORISATION

Choose three of the Beatitudes and learn them by heart.

THE CAPUCHIN DAY CENTRE FOR HOMELESS PEOPLE

In 1969 Brother Kevin Crowley founded the Capuchin Day Centre for Homeless People in Bow Street, Dublin. Today, with the help of many volunteers, the Centre provides over 700 meals each day and over 1,500 food parcels each Wednesday to the homeless and poor of Dublin.

The Capuchin Day Centre for Homeless People is an example of the Beatitudes in action. In other words, the good work that takes place at this Centre shows the values and attitudes that Jesus taught being put into practice. The Centre brings happiness to those who provide the service, as well as to those who avail of it – just as Jesus promised would happen when people respond with love to one another.

THINK ABOUT IT …

- Which Beatitudes do you think you would see in action on a visit to the Capuchin Day Centre?

THIS WEEK
The children learned that their attitudes can affect their actions and the way they relate to others. Good attitudes tend to produce good behaviours towards others, whereas bad attitudes often lead to bad actions. In the Sermon on the Mount, Jesus gave us the Beatitudes – a set of good attitudes and values that he wants his followers to live by. The Beatitudes, along with the Ten Commandments and the New Commandment, can help us to live good lives. If we live according to these, we will be happy and we will bring happiness to others.

Read the poem 'Beatitudes' together.

Beatitudes
If you can hold great riches,
Never letting them hold you;
If you can hear your praises being sung
And still give God his due;

If you can help the slow and weak
And raise the one who falls,
And quickly come with helping hand
When anybody calls;

If you can have a heart that's free
From selfishness and sin,
And keep that heart so God's great light
May shine more strongly in;

If you can give forgiveness
To the one who hurt your heart;
If you can build a bridge and bring
Together those apart;

If you can say – this thing is wrong
Or that is right to do,
And stand your ground though other hearts
Would pain and punish you;

If you can be a friend to all,
To all be strong and true,
Then God who made the world
Will make his Kingdom come in you.

DID YOU KNOW?

BEATITUDE = BE + ATTITUDE. In other words, each Beatitude teaches us how we should 'be' in the world as followers of Jesus.

TIME TOGETHER

Respond and Share
Think about ways in which people in your family already live the Beatitudes – the 'Be' attitudes that Jesus taught us! Write about one of those ways in your Religious Education journal. Then share what you have written with your parent or guardian.

Pray Together
Jesus, our friend and teacher, help us to live according to your Beatitudes.
Help us to follow you, no matter the cost. Amen.

Begin!
Begin today to consider how you could live your life according to the Beatitudes.

THIS WEEK IN SCHOOL

You are invited to think about:

- How God, human beings and the natural world are connected
- How human actions contribute to the destruction of the earth
- How we can respect and care for the earth, as God asked us to

KEY WORDS

Evolution: The process by which different organisms and life forms are thought to have developed over the course of the earth's history.

Encyclical: A letter written by the Pope to all the members of the Church throughout the world.

Laudato Si': An Italian phrase meaning 'Praise be to you'. *Laudato Si'* is the name of a letter (encyclical) written by Pope Francis and addressed to 'every person living on this planet'.

THEME 6: SOCIAL JUSTICE | LESSON 3

We Are Called to Care for Our Common Home

ALL LIFE ON EARTH IS CONNECTED

The earliest forms of life began on planet Earth around 3.8 billion years ago. Human life came much later. Life in all its forms has grown and developed ever since – a process that we call **evolution**.

As far back as the nineteenth century, scientists such as Charles Darwin started to realise that all living things and all species are connected in a great web of life. Since then, scientists have continued to gather evidence to show the connections that exist between all living things on earth.

As Christians, we accept that the world evolved over the centuries, while at the same time recognising that God is the source of *all* life. The saints were very aware of this. For example, St Francis of Assisi called birds, fish, sheep, the moon and the stars his 'brothers and sisters'.

THINK ABOUT IT ...

- How might people's attitude to caring for the earth and all its creatures change if we looked upon every living creature as our 'brother and sister' – as St Francis of Assisi did?

St Francis of Assisi Preaching to the Birds by Giotto (c. 1300)

Read the following account of the creation of the world and of the different living creatures that inhabit the world as it is told in the Book of Genesis in the Bible.

The Story of Creation (Adapted from Genesis 1:1-31)

In the beginning, there was nothing. There was no sky, no sun, no moon and no stars. There was just water moving around in a dark, empty space. God did not want things to be this way. So God said, 'Let there be light!' – and light appeared. God called the light 'day' and the darkness 'night'.

Then God decided to separate the water in the white clouds above from the water on the earth below. So God created the sky.

Then God said, 'Let dry land appear.' And it happened. Dry land appeared from underneath the water. God named the dry land 'earth' and the water that was gathered together 'sea'.

Then God said, 'Let all kinds of plants grow on the earth.' And it happened. There was every kind of plant that you could imagine! God looked at everything he had made: the light, the sky, the sea, the land and the plants. God was pleased with all that he had made. It was good.

Next, God made the bright, warm sun in the sky to shine during the day. After that, God made the glowing moon and the twinkling stars to shine at night. Now the sky was not bare – there would always be something in it! God was pleased with what he saw.

Then God said, 'Let the water be filled with all kinds of creatures. And let beautiful birds fly in the sky above the earth.' So God created amazing animals to live in the water, and all kinds of birds to fly across the sky. God looked at all he had made: the sun, the moon and the stars, the creatures of the sea and the creatures of the air. God was pleased with everything. It was all good.

But God knew that the world needed something else – something special. The world needed something that was *very* good. So, God made people. God wanted the people to care for the fish and the birds and the animals, and God wanted them to look after one another too. God made the people to be like himself. They would be good and kind and loving. They would all be good at different things but, together, they would use the things that they were good at to take care of the world. When God saw all of this, he knew that it wasn't just good. People were special. It was very good.

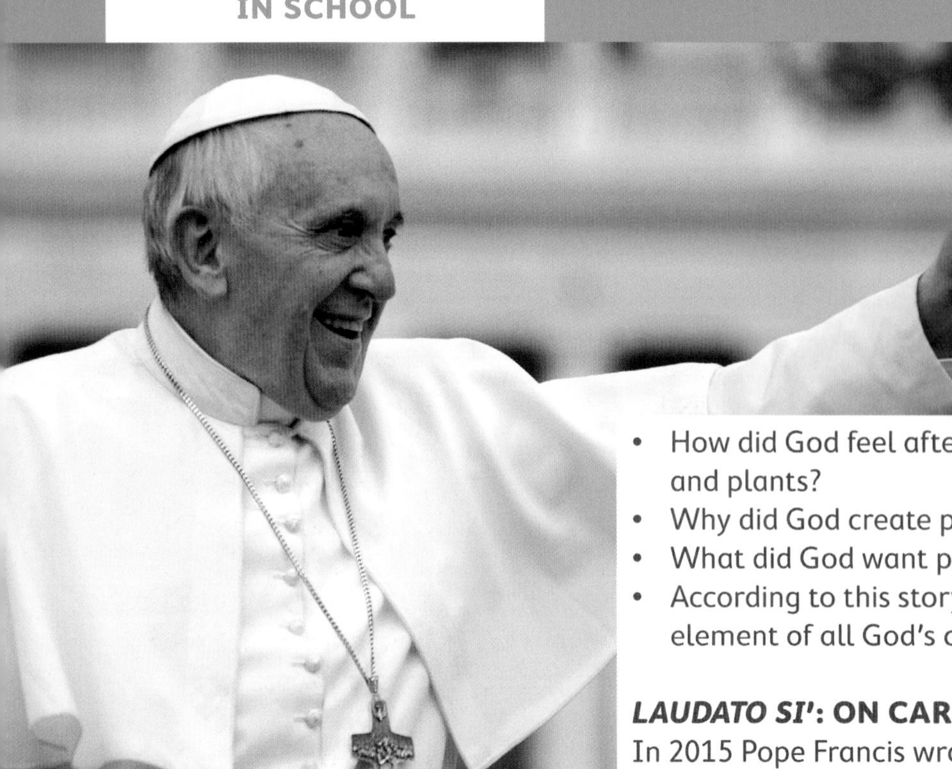

- How did God feel after creating the light, sky, sea, land and plants?
- Why did God create people?
- What did God want people to do?
- According to this story, why are people the most special element of all God's creation?

LAUDATO SI': ON CARE FOR OUR COMMON HOME

In 2015 Pope Francis wrote an important letter, called an **encyclical**, to every person on the planet. He called the letter ***Laudato Si'***, which is an old Italian phrase that means 'Praise be to you'.

In *Laudato Si'* Pope Francis reminds us that the earth, which he calls 'our common home', is God's gift to us. It is full of beauty and wonder, and it belongs to everyone. The Pope also tells us that the earth has never been so badly treated and damaged as it is now. Human activities such as pollution of the environment, careless disposal of waste, and also climate change and the lack of clean water, all threaten our planet.

But Pope Francis reassures us that it is not too late – we *can* change our behaviour, and we *can* make a new start in caring for our planet and for all the creatures that live on it.

Pope Francis urges the whole human family to work together to care for our planet. He asks us to take simple actions to change our behaviour and to show our love for our planet and for one another. When we adopt the right attitude and look upon the earth as 'our common home', we will have a new care and respect for it, and look after it as God asked us to.

JOURNAL EXERCISE

- What do you think of Pope Francis' letter to the world, reminding us of the need to care for the earth, 'our common home'? Do you agree with him? Write your thoughts on this in your Religious Education journal. Mention some of the things you think people could do to take better care of the earth.

FOR MEMORISATION

Creator God,
you made the world and
everything in it.
Praise be to you!

THIS WEEK

The children recalled the story of creation in the Book of Genesis, and how God gave humans the responsibility to care for the earth and all its creatures. Instead, as Pope Francis reminds us in his encyclical letter *Laudato Si': On Care for Our Common Home,* people have exploited and damaged the earth and its resources. The Pope urges us to look upon the world as 'our common home' and to respect and care for it as God asked us to. We have a responsibility to take care of the world not only for ourselves but for the generations to come.

Read the poem 'Environmental Change' together. A boy named Patrick Barrett from County Mayo wrote this poem for a poetry competition run by Trócaire in 2015.

Environmental Change

Temperatures are rising,
Sea levels are rising too,
I don't own a canoe,
So what do you suggest I do?

I could move to Scandinavia,
And live amongst the ice and snow,
But if the temperatures keep rising,
All of that too will go.

I suppose I could recycle,
Turn the lights off as I go,
Maybe plant a tree or two.
It might help, you never know.

Environmental change is happening,
It is something we can't outrun.
Can we explain to our children
Just what we have done?

DID YOU KNOW?

Science and Sacred Scripture are complementary rather than contradictory in helping us to understand the wonder of God's creation.

TIME TOGETHER

Chat Together
Talk about the simple steps that you can take to care for our planet, such as reducing the amount of paper you use, reducing food waste, recycling, and using less water.

Respond and Share
Make a list of three things you will do in your home to help to take care of our planet. Share what you have written with your parent or guardian.

Pray Together
Loving God, help us to care for our planet and everything on it as you asked us to. Amen.

Be Responsible
Make a commitment to always reduce, reuse, recycle or repair instead of being wasteful.

THIS WEEK IN SCHOOL

You are invited to think about:

- How Jesus must have felt at each stage of his final journey to his death
- The key moments of Jesus' final journey that are marked by the Stations of the Cross
- How you might celebrate Holy Week this year

KEY WORDS

The Passion: The final days in the life of Jesus, beginning with his entrance into Jerusalem and ending with his crucifixion on the hill of Calvary.

Garden of Gethsemane: The garden at the foot of the Mount of Olives, where Jesus went to pray after the Last Supper.

Via Dolorosa: A street within the Old City of Jerusalem, believed to be the path that Jesus walked on the way to his crucifixion.

Stations of the Cross: The story of Jesus' final journey to his death on the Cross is recorded in art form in the fourteen Stations of the Cross. Each Station marks a point on that journey.

Golgotha: The name of the hill on which Jesus was crucified. Also known as Calvary.

THEME 7: HOLY WEEK AND EASTER | LESSON 1

Walking in the Footsteps of Jesus

JESUS' FINAL JOURNEY

Christians sometimes refer to the final days in the life of Jesus as the **Passion**. Below are some images and descriptions from that final journey. Pilgrims to Jerusalem can still see all of these places that are associated with Jesus.

The Walls of Jerusalem

The city of Jerusalem has been surrounded by walls since ancient times. The walls were built to defend the city against its enemies. The walls were destroyed and rebuilt several times over thousands of years. When Jesus entered the city of Jerusalem for the last time, he would have entered through a gate similar to the one shown here. We remember that event on Palm Sunday.

THINK ABOUT IT ...

- Imagine how Jesus felt when he saw the crowds waving palm branches and shouting, 'Praise God! God bless him who comes in the name of the Lord!'

The Cenacle

According to tradition, this is the room where Jesus celebrated the Last Supper with his apostles, an event that we remember on Holy Thursday. It is also believed that this is the room where the Holy Spirit came upon the apostles on the Feast of Pentecost.

THINK ABOUT IT ...

- Imagine how Jesus felt as he celebrated the Last Supper with his apostles, knowing that he would soon be put to death.

The Garden of Gethsemane

The **Garden of Gethsemane** is located near the foot of the Mount of Olives. It is the place where Jesus went to pray after the Last Supper. It was here that Jesus was arrested by Roman soldiers, having been betrayed by his friend and follower, Judas Iscariot.

THINK ABOUT IT ...

- Imagine how Jesus felt when Judas betrayed him.

The Church of St Peter in Gallicantu

After Jesus was arrested, he was taken to the home of Caiaphas, the High Priest. While he was being questioned there, his friend Peter stood outside in the courtyard and denied three times that he even knew Jesus. That event took place at the site where the Church of St Peter now stands. Under the church is the dungeon thought to be the place where Jesus spent the night before he died.

THINK ABOUT IT ...

- Imagine how Jesus felt when Peter denied that he even knew him.

The Citadel

The picture shows the remains of the Citadel, Herod the Great's Palace in the city of Jerusalem, which scholars believe is the place where Jesus was condemned to death by Pilate.

Today, visitors also call to the Chapel of the Condemnation, which is believed to be the site where Jesus was given his Cross.

THINK ABOUT IT ...

- Does seeing pictures of these places on Jesus' final journey help you to understand better the story of what happened during Holy Week?

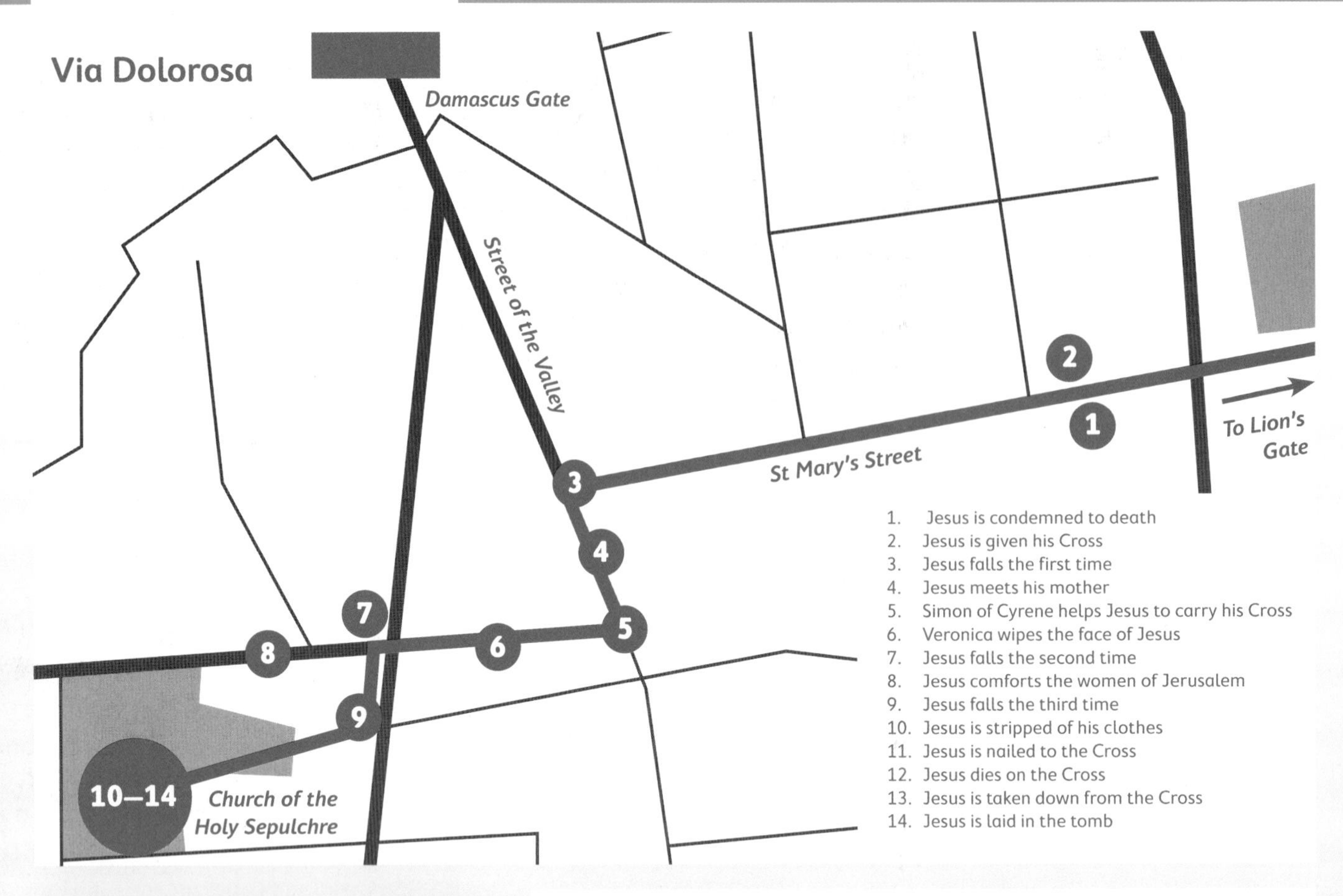

Marker of the 8th Station on the Via Dolorosa, Jerusalem

The Via Dolorosa

The **Via Dolorosa** is a street within the Old City of Jerusalem that is believed to be the path Jesus walked on the way to his crucifixion. The words 'Via Dolorosa' mean 'Way of Grief'. This path is also known as the Way of the Cross. There are fourteen stops or 'stations' along the way to the place where Jesus was laid in the tomb. Stations 10-13 mark a hill known as **Golgotha**, also called Calvary, where Jesus was nailed to the Cross and then died.

On Good Friday each year, thousands of people gather in Jerusalem to walk and pray the Via Dolorosa. Thousands more join the Pope in the Colosseum in Rome, where he leads prayers based on each of the **Stations of the Cross**.

In almost every Catholic Church, fourteen Stations of the Cross are displayed on the walls. On Good Friday and on other days throughout the year, people walk from Station to Station as though they, too, are walking the Via Dolorosa. They remember what happened at each point on Jesus' final journey and the people he met along the way. They also say some prayers at each Station.

FOR MEMORISATION

Learn the fourteen Stations of the Cross (listed on next page)

JOURNAL EXERCISE

- Choose five Stations of the Cross (*listed on next page*) and imagine how Jesus felt at each of those moments. Write a sentence about each one in your Religious Education journal.

AT HOME

THIS WEEK

The children remembered the events of Holy Week, beginning with the day we now call Palm Sunday, when Jesus entered the city of Jerusalem riding on a donkey. Later that week Jesus celebrated his final meal with his friends. He was then betrayed by one of those friends and arrested in the Garden of Gethsemane. From there, Jesus was taken to the home of Caiaphas, the Jewish High Priest, and then to the palace of the Roman Governor, Pilate, where he was sentenced to death. The fourteen Stations of the Cross mark the way from Pilate's palace to the hill where Jesus was crucified.

Read the names of the fourteen Stations of the Cross together.

1. Jesus is condemned to death
2. Jesus is given his Cross
3. Jesus falls the first time
4. Jesus meets his mother
5. Simon of Cyrene helps Jesus to carry his Cross
6. Veronica wipes the face of Jesus
7. Jesus falls the second time
8. Jesus comforts the women of Jerusalem
9. Jesus falls the third time
10. Jesus is stripped of his clothes
11. Jesus is nailed to the Cross
12. Jesus dies on the Cross
13. Jesus is taken down from the Cross
14. Jesus is laid in the tomb

DID YOU KNOW?

Pilgrims to Jerusalem can still see all of the places associated with Jesus, including the path he took on the way to his death.

TIME TOGETHER

Chat Together
Talk about how you and your family might celebrate Holy Week this year.

Research and Share
Find out when the Stations of the Cross will be prayed in your local church this Good Friday. Consider inviting your parent or guardian to accompany you to the Stations.

Pray Together
Dearest Jesus, you gave your life for us.
Help us to be very grateful for this sacrifice of love.
Help us to appreciate the sacrifices that others make for us out of love. Amen.

Be Prayerful
As you reflect on the events of Holy Week, be as prayerful as you can and remember all that Jesus suffered out of love for us.

THIS WEEK IN SCHOOL

You are invited to think about:

- How belief in God, or **faith**, differs from other beliefs
- The post-Resurrection appearances of Jesus
- Jesus is both divine and human
- How the Resurrection teaches us that Jesus is God
- The statements of belief we make when we pray the *Nicene Creed*

KEY WORDS

Faith: Belief in God.

Nicene Creed: A creed is a statement of what a person believes. The *Nicene Creed* is a statement of what Catholics believe. It is named after Nicaea (in present-day Turkey), where it was written.

THEME 7: HOLY WEEK AND EASTER | LESSON 2

'My Lord and My God'

GOSPEL ACCOUNTS OF THE RESURRECTION OF JESUS

There are three accounts in the Gospels of how the apostles reacted to Jesus' Resurrection. Here is the story of the empty tomb as it is told in the Gospel according to John.

The Empty Tomb (John 20:1-10)

Early on Sunday morning, while it was still dark, Mary Magdalene went to the tomb and saw that the stone had been taken away from the entrance. She went running to Simon Peter and the other disciple, whom Jesus loved, and told them, 'They have taken the Lord from the tomb, and we don't know where they have put him!'

Then Peter and the other disciple went to the tomb. The two of them were running, but the other disciple ran faster than Peter and reached the tomb first. He bent over and saw the linen cloths, but he did not go in. Behind him came Simon Peter, and he went straight into the tomb. He saw the linen cloths lying there and the cloth which had been around Jesus' head. It was not lying with the linen cloths but was rolled up by itself. Then the other disciple, who had reached the tomb first, also went in; he saw and believed. (They still did not understand the scripture which said that he must rise from death.) Then the disciples went back home.

- Who was the first person to discover the empty tomb?
- What did Mary Magdalene say to Simon Peter and the other disciple about what had happened?
- Which of the two disciples went into the tomb first? And what did he find?
- How did the second disciple react when he saw the empty tomb?
- Where did the disciples go after that?

THINK ABOUT IT...

- Think about how you might have felt if, like Mary Magdalene, you had been the first person to discover the tomb of Jesus empty.

Now read the story of the Risen Jesus appearing to Mary Magdalene, which is also in the Gospel according to John.

Jesus Appears to Mary Magdalene (John 20:11-18)

Mary stood crying outside the tomb. While she was still crying, she bent over and looked in the tomb and saw two angels there dressed in white, sitting where the body of Jesus had been, one at the head and the other at the feet. 'Woman, why are you crying?' they asked her.

She answered, 'They have taken my Lord away, and I do not know where they have put him!'

Then she turned around and saw Jesus standing there, but she did not know that it was Jesus. 'Woman, why are you crying?' Jesus asked her. 'Who is it that you are looking for?'

She thought he was the gardener, so she said to him, 'If you took him away, sir, tell me where you have put him, and I will go and get him.'

Jesus said to her, 'Mary!'

She turned towards him and said in Hebrew, 'Rabboni!' (This means 'Teacher.')

'Do not hold on to me,' Jesus told her, 'because I have not yet gone back up to the Father. But go to my brothers and tell them that I am returning to him who is my Father and their Father, my God and their God.'

So Mary Magdalene went and told the disciples that she had seen the Lord and related to them what he had told her.

- Why was Mary Magdalene crying?
- Who did Mary see first when she looked into the tomb?
- Who did Mary think the Risen Jesus was when she saw him?
- What did Mary say to the Risen Jesus when she realised who he was?
- What did the Risen Jesus tell Mary about where he was going, and what did he ask Mary to do?
- What did Mary do after she had spoken to the Risen Jesus?

The Gospel according to John also contains the following account of the Risen Jesus appearing to his disciples.

Jesus Appears to His Disciples (John 20:19-20, 24-29)

It was late that Sunday evening, and the disciples were gathered together behind locked doors, because they were afraid of the Jewish authorities. Then Jesus came and stood among them. 'Peace be with you,' he said. After saying this, he showed them his hands and his side. The disciples were filled with joy at seeing the Lord ...

One of the twelve disciples, Thomas (called the Twin), was not with them when Jesus came. So the other disciples told him, 'We have seen the Lord!'

Thomas said to them, 'Unless I see the scars of the nails in his hands and put my finger on those scars and my hand in his side, I will not believe.'

A week later the disciples were together again indoors, and Thomas was with them. The doors were locked, but Jesus came and stood among them and said, 'Peace be with you.' Then he said to Thomas, 'Put your finger here, and look at my hands; then reach out your hand and put it in my side. Stop your doubting, and believe!'

Thomas answered him, 'My Lord and my God!'

Jesus said to him, 'Do you believe because you see me? How happy are those who believe without seeing me!'

- Where were the disciples gathered, and why had they gathered there?
- What did the Risen Jesus say when he appeared among them?
- Which of the disciples refused to believe that it was the Risen Jesus until he had proof?
- What did Thomas say when the other disciples told him that they had seen the Lord?
- What did Thomas say when the Risen Jesus appeared the second time and showed him proof of who he was?

THINK ABOUT IT ...

- Do you think you would have been doubtful, like Thomas was, or do you think you would have believed without needing proof, as the other disciples did?

JOURNAL EXERCISE

- Read the *Nicene Creed*, which you will find on page 146 of this book. Then write in your journal one thing that it says about God the Father, God the Son (Jesus), and God the Holy Spirit, and one thing that it says about the Church.

FOR MEMORISATION

Learn the *Nicene Creed.*

AT HOME

THIS WEEK

The children explored three stories from the Gospels that tell us how the disciples of Jesus reacted to the news of his Resurrection. The first disciples to witness the empty tomb thought that Jesus' body had been stolen. It was only when Mary Magdalene saw the Risen Jesus for herself that she realised he had risen. Thomas also didn't believe until he saw proof. But once they knew that Jesus had really come back to life, they began to understand that he was not just a human being and not just the Messiah – Jesus was God.

The *Nicene Creed* is a statement of what Catholics believe. This prayer is usually prayed at Mass after the homily. There are four distinct parts to the *Nicene Creed*: relating to God the Father, to Jesus, to the Holy Spirit and to the Church. Each part lists the things we believe about each of these. Pray the first two parts of the *Nicene Creed* together now. (You will find the full prayer on page 146 of this book.)

Nicene Creed

I believe in one God,
the Father almighty,
maker of heaven and earth,
of all things visible and invisible.

I believe in one Lord Jesus Christ,
the Only Begotten Son of God,
born of the Father before all ages.
God from God, Light from Light,
true God from true God,
begotten, not made, consubstantial with the Father;
through him all things were made.
For us men and for our salvation
he came down from heaven,
and by the Holy Spirit was incarnate of the Virgin Mary,
and became man.

For our sake he was crucified under Pontius Pilate,
he suffered death and was buried,
and rose again on the third day
in accordance with the Scriptures.
He ascended into heaven
and is seated at the right hand of the Father.

He will come again in glory
to judge the living and the dead
and his kingdom will have no end.

DID YOU KNOW?

The Resurrection teaches us that Jesus is God.

TIME TOGETHER

Chat Together

Chat together about how it can sometimes be difficult to have **faith**. Things may happen to us that cause us to question our faith. Jesus assures us that those who believe 'without seeing' are truly blessed.

Respond and Share

Do you know someone who has great faith? Write about that person in your Religious Education journal. Then share what you have written with your parent or guardian.

Be Confident

Sometimes people might try to convince you that you are wrong to believe in God. Be confident in what you know is true. Pray to God for help to remain strong in your faith.

THIS WEEK IN SCHOOL

You are invited to think about:

- How the Holy Spirit helped the apostles in their work
- How the same Holy Spirit comes to us in Baptism to help us to live as Jesus asked
- The ways in which you might continue the work that Jesus began while he was on earth

KEY WORDS

Preach: Teach.

Mission: A task or job. Jesus' mission was to tell people about God and to teach them how to live in love of God and of others.

Missionaries: People who continue the mission of Jesus by sharing the Good News.

THEME 7: HOLY WEEK AND EASTER | LESSON 3

Jesus' Work Continues Today

ALL DIFFERENT, YET ALL EQUAL IN GOD'S EYES!

There are about 7.5 billion people living on our planet – that's 7,500,000,000! Even more amazingly, no two people are exactly alike. Even identical twins are different in some ways. Each and every person has different qualities and different abilities. We are all good at different things.

Think about your own family and friends:

- Which of them are trustworthy and reliable?
- Which of them are fun to be with?
- How many of them are kind and helpful?
- Who is good at school work?
- Who is sporty?
- Who is artistic?

Yes, we are all different – and God loves each one of us.

JOURNAL EXERCISE

- Write your name in the middle of a new page in your Religious Education journal and draw a circle around it. Then draw lines coming from that circle and pointing to all the positive things that people might say about you – perhaps that you are a good listener, that you are very kind, that you are funny, and so on.

JESUS CHOOSES THE TWELVE APOSTLES

When Jesus was choosing the twelve apostles, he had to decide which of his followers would be the best people for the work that he wanted them to do. They would be the ones who would continue building the Kingdom of God on earth after he had returned to his Father in heaven. The Gospels of Mark and Matthew record what Jesus said to his apostles when he chose them and sent them out to **preach**; in other words, to teach people about God.

Jesus Chooses the Twelve Apostles (Mark 3:13-14, Matthew 10:11-12, 14, 16, 40, 42)

Then Jesus went up a hill and called to himself the men he wanted. They came to him, and he chose twelve, whom he named apostles. 'I have chosen you to be with me,' he told them. 'I will also send you out to preach' ...

'When you come to a town or village, go in and look for someone who is willing to welcome you, and stay with him until you leave that place. When you go into a house, say, "Peace be with you."... And if some home or town will not welcome you or listen to you, then leave that place and shake the dust off your feet.'

'Listen! I am sending you out just like sheep to a pack of wolves. You must be as cautious as snakes and as gentle as doves.'

'Whoever welcomes you welcomes me; and whoever welcomes me welcomes the one who sent me ... You can be sure that whoever gives even a drink of cold water to one of the least of these my followers because he is my follower, will certainly receive a reward.'

- How many people did Jesus choose as his apostles, and what did he want them to do?
- What did Jesus tell the apostles to do when they entered a town or village?
- What did Jesus say they should do if they came to a home or town that was not welcoming?
- What did Jesus compare their task to? And what advice did he give them about how they should approach it?
- What did Jesus say about those who would welcome the apostles and the message they brought?

Jesus knew that what he was asking his apostles to do would be difficult. So he promised to send a Helper to assist them in their task. This promise is recorded in the Gospel according to John.

The Promise of the Holy Spirit (John 14:15-17, 26)

[Jesus said] 'If you love me, you will obey my commandments. I will ask the Father, and he will give you another Helper, who will stay with you forever. He is the Spirit, who reveals the truth about God … You know him, because he remains with you and is in you.'

'The Helper, the Holy Spirit, whom the Father will send in my name, will teach you everything and make you remember all that I have told you.'

- Who did Jesus say he would ask to send a Helper to his apostles and other disciples?
- Who was this Helper?
- What did Jesus say the Helper would do?

THE HOLY SPIRIT COMES TO US IN BAPTISM AND CONFIRMATION

Just as Jesus sent the Holy Spirit to his apostles, and to the other disciples who came after them, to help them in their work, Jesus also sent the Holy Spirit to us at our Baptism, to help us to live as his followers. The Holy Spirit remains with us as we live in the way Jesus asked by loving God and loving others. At our Confirmation the Holy Spirit comes to us again and strengthens us to take on even more of the work that Jesus has asked us to do.

FOR MEMORISATION

Jesus said: 'If you love me, you will obey my commandments. I will ask the Father, and he will give you another Helper, who will stay with you forever.' (John 14:15-16)

THINK ABOUT IT …

- Think about some of the things you can do to continue the work Jesus began when he was on earth – the work of building a world that is peaceful and loving, where everyone is treated equally and fairly, where everyone has what they need to live a normal and healthy life, and where no one is left out or ignored.

NET MINISTRIES

The Holy Spirit still works through lots of people and groups who do God's work in the world today. One of those groups is called NET Ministries. NET stands for National Evangelisation Teams. NET Ministries Ireland is an organisation of young Catholic **missionaries** who share the Gospel message with children and young adults in churches, schools and parishes all across Ireland.

AT HOME

THIS WEEK

The children recalled that Jesus chose twelve apostles to continue his work on earth after he returned to his Father in heaven. Jesus told the twelve that this would not be an easy task. He promised them that he would ask God the Father to send the Holy Spirit to help them. That same Holy Spirit comes to every Christian at their Baptism. The Holy Spirit helps us to continue the work of Jesus today and to live in the way Jesus modelled for us.

Pray this *Prayer to the Holy Spirit* together:

> Holy Spirit, I want to do what is right. Help me.
> Holy Spirit, I want to live like Jesus. Guide me.
> Holy Spirit, I want to pray like Jesus. Teach me.

DID YOU KNOW?

The Holy Spirit comes to us in the Sacrament of Baptism, and again at our Confirmation.

TIME TOGETHER

Chat Together
Talk about people whom you know who show by the way they live that they are followers of Jesus. Consider the ways in which you and your family could do the same.

Respond and Share
Decide on one thing that your family could do to show that you are followers of Jesus. Write about this in your Religious Education journal. Then share what you have written with your parent or guardian.

Be Courageous
Be courageous in living as a true follower of Jesus.

THIS WEEK IN SCHOOL

You are invited to think about:

- What you already know about the Holy Spirit
- How you experience the Holy Spirit at work in your life
- How you are called to continue the mission of Jesus

KEY WORDS

Symbol: Something that has meaning and value beyond its outward appearance.

Mission: A task or job. Jesus' mission was to tell people about God and to teach them how to live in love of God and of others.

THEME 8: THE HOLY SPIRIT | LESSON 1

The Holy Spirit

RECALL THE STORY: 'AN INDIAN LEGEND'

- Each of the men in the story had heard different things about what an elephant is like. How many of those things can you remember?
- Can you remember what each of the men thought about what an elephant is like after they had a chance to touch the animal?

THE HOLY SPIRIT

Like the men in the story who couldn't see the elephant, we cannot see the Holy Spirit. Nor can we touch the Holy Spirit the way the men were able to touch the elephant. We learn about the Holy Spirit from many different sources, especially from the words and actions of Jesus. But we also learn about the Holy Spirit from our own experience of the Spirit at work in us. When we want to describe the Holy Spirit, we often use **symbols**, like fire, a dove and wind.

THE BAPTISM OF JESUS

When he was thirty years of age, Jesus was baptised by John the Baptist in the River Jordan. The story of Jesus' baptism is told in all four Gospels. The Holy Spirit came upon Jesus at his baptism. The same Holy Spirit came to you when you were baptised. Here is the account of Jesus' baptism from the Gospel according to Matthew.

The Baptism of Jesus (Matthew 3:13-17)

At that time Jesus arrived from Galilee and came to John at the Jordan to be baptised by him. But John tried to make him change his mind. 'I ought to be baptised by you,' John said, 'and yet you have come to me!'

But Jesus answered him, 'Let it be so for now. For in this way we shall do all that God requires.' So John agreed.

As soon as Jesus was baptised, he came up out of the water. Then heaven was opened to him, and he saw the Spirit of God coming down like a dove and lighting on him. Then a voice said from heaven, 'This is my own dear Son, with whom I am pleased.'

THINK ABOUT IT ...

- Why do you think Jesus wanted to be baptised by John?
- How do you imagine Jesus felt after John had baptised him?

JESUS, FILLED WITH THE SPIRIT, SPEAKS OUT

The Gospel according to Luke describes the effect Jesus had on those around him when he returned home to Nazareth after his baptism and read aloud from the Book of Isaiah in the synagogue.

The Spirit of the Lord (Luke 4:16-22)

Then Jesus went to Nazareth, where he had been brought up, and on the Sabbath he went as usual to the synagogue. He stood up to read the Scriptures and was handed the book of the prophet Isaiah. He unrolled the scroll and found the place where it is written,

'The Spirit of the Lord is upon me,
because he has chosen me to bring good news to the poor.
He has sent me to proclaim liberty to the captives
and recovery of sight to the blind,
to set free the oppressed
and announce that the time has come
when the Lord will save his people.'

Jesus rolled up the scroll, gave it back to the attendant, and sat down. All the people in the synagogue had their eyes fixed on him, as he said to them, 'This passage of scripture has come true today, as you heard it being read.'

They were all well impressed with him and marvelled at the eloquence of the words that he spoke.

- Which part of the Bible did Jesus read?
- What were the five things that the Spirit of the Lord had said should be done?
- What did Jesus mean when he said, 'This passage of scripture has come true today, as you heard it being read'?
- How did the people react to what Jesus said?

THINK ABOUT IT ...

- Would you have been impressed by Jesus' words if you had been there in the synagogue that day? What do you think about the message that he read out and the other things he said?

FOR MEMORISATION

'The Spirit of the Lord is upon me,
because he has chosen me to bring good news to the poor.' (Luke 4:18)

WE CONTINUE JESUS' MISSION

Before Jesus returned to his Father in heaven, he instructed his friends to carry on his **mission**, which was to bring God's love to all people. We, too, are called to continue the mission of Jesus in our day-to-day lives by loving our neighbour as Jesus did, especially when our neighbour is poor, or ignored by others, or not seen to be as important as others in our community.

THINK ABOUT IT ...

- How do you feel about being called to continue the mission of Jesus?

AT HOME

THIS WEEK

The children recalled what they already know about the Holy Spirit. They were reminded that, while we cannot see or touch the Holy Spirit, we can feel and experience the Spirit at work in our lives and in the lives of others. We can also learn about the Holy Spirit from the life of Jesus – from the things he said and the way he interacted with people. The children also learned that the Church uses many symbols to describe the presence and action of the Holy Spirit in the world, such as fire, wind and the symbol of a dove.

Read this verse of the song 'Go Tell Everyone' together.

He sent me to bring the Good News to the poor,
Tell prisoners that they are prisoners no more,
Tell blind people that they can see,
And set the downtrodden free,
And go tell everyone
The news that the Kingdom of God has come.

DID YOU KNOW?

Jesus fulfilled the words that were written by the prophet Isaiah. Isaiah lived about eight hundred years before Jesus was born.

TIME TOGETHER

Chat Together

Think about some of the things that Jesus did with the help of the Holy Spirit – forgiving sins, healing people who were sick and disabled, and telling people about God and God's kingdom. Do you know any people who act like Jesus?

Respond and Share

In your Religious Education journal, describe someone who does great things like Jesus did when he was filled with the Spirit. Include a photo or draw a picture of them. Share your reflection with your parent or guardian.

Be Spirit-filled

Allow the Holy Spirit to fill your life so that you can live as a true follower of Jesus.

THEME 8: THE HOLY SPIRIT | LESSON 2

The Gifts of the Holy Spirit

THIS WEEK IN SCHOOL

You are invited to think about:

- The difficulties young people face as they try to live as true followers of Jesus
- The seven gifts of the Holy Spirit and how they help people to live the Christian life
- Examples of people who show the gifts of the Holy Spirit at work in their lives

KEY WORDS

Advocate: A title for the Holy Spirit. The word describes someone who helps or comes to the aid of another.

Paraclete: Another title for the Holy Spirit. Jesus used this title to describe the Holy Spirit. It means a consoler, counsellor or advocate.

Gifts of the Holy Spirit: Wisdom, Understanding, Right Judgement [*Counsel*], Courage [*Fortitude*], Knowledge, Reverence [*Piety*], and Wonder and Awe in God's presence [*Fear of the Lord*].

JESUS PROMISED TO SEND A HELPER TO HIS FOLLOWERS

Jesus recognised how difficult it can be to live the Christian life. Before he returned to his Father in heaven, Jesus promised his followers a Helper, or **Advocate**, who would support them in their efforts and who would be with them at all times to guide them. This Helper was the Holy Spirit.

- Read again the passage from the Gospel according to John where Jesus made this promise. The passage is on page 80 of this book.

NAMES FOR THE HOLY SPIRIT

In the passage on page 80 from the Gospel according to John, Jesus used the title 'Helper' to describe the Holy Spirit. 'Helper' is just one of the many titles used in the Bible to describe the Holy Spirit. Here are some of the other titles for the Holy Spirit:

'Spirit of God' **'Spirit of Christ'**
'Spirit of Truth' **'Paraclete'** **'Advocate',**
'Teacher' **'Guide'** **'Gift of God Most High'**

JOURNAL EXERCISE

- Write some of these titles for the Holy Spirit on a page of your Religious Education journal and decorate it.

THE SEVEN GIFTS OF THE HOLY SPIRIT

God gives us the gift of the Holy Spirit at our Baptism. The Holy Spirit offers us seven gifts to help us to live as followers of Jesus. At our Confirmation, the Holy Spirit increases the seven gifts in us.

The seven **gifts of the Holy Spirit** are:

Wisdom

The Holy Spirit's gift of Wisdom helps people to have a deep understanding of God and to value the things of God. People who draw on the gift of Wisdom have the ability to recognise that material things or worldly goods are not as important as spiritual things (things that relate to God). The material things of this world are only temporary – unlike God, who is everlasting or eternal.

Understanding

The Holy Spirit's gift of Understanding helps Christians to know God better. We can never fully know God because God is a mystery that our human minds can never fully understand. But we can come to understand many things about God through the gift of Understanding.

Right Judgement [*Counsel*]

Through the gift of Right Judgement the Holy Spirit inspires and guides Christians to make the right decisions and to do the right thing, particularly in difficult situations where it isn't always easy to know the right thing to do and to choose to do it.

Courage [*Fortitude*]

The Holy Spirit's gift of Courage gives Christians the strength to do God's will and to stand up for what is right. Sometimes this may not be the popular or easy thing to do, and it can often mean being rejected or criticised or even harmed.

Knowledge

The Holy Spirit's gift of Knowledge helps Christians to know and understand God's truth and God's plan for us in a deeper way. Full knowledge of God can only come about by God revealing certain truths to us – which we call Divine Revelation.

Reverence [*Piety*]

The Holy Spirit's gift of Reverence helps Christians to show their love for God. People filled with this gift have a deep respect for God and they desire to show this by taking part in the Church's public liturgies, and by praying at other times on their own.

Wonder and Awe in God's presence [*Fear of the Lord*]

The Holy Spirit's gift of Wonder and Awe in God's presence helps Christians to know how great God is. This gift helps people to recognise the wonders of God's creation and to know that God alone is perfect.

FOR MEMORISATION

The seven gifts of the Holy Spirit are: Wisdom, Understanding, Right Judgement [*Counsel*], Courage [*Fortitude*], Knowledge, Reverence [*Piety*], and Wonder and Awe in God's presence [*Fear of the Lord*].

JOURNAL EXERCISE

- Imagine that it is the day of your Confirmation and you receive the gifts of the Holy Spirit. Choose the gift that you like best and record in your Religious Education journal how you hope to use it. You may use words, pictures or symbols to convey your message.

THIS WEEK

The children learned that all Christians receive the gift of the Holy Spirit in Baptism to help them face the difficulties they will meet in their daily lives as they try to follow the way of Jesus. We helped the children to name some of the challenges they themselves encounter that prevent them from living in ways that bring them closer to God. The children also learned that the Holy Spirit gives us seven gifts at our Confirmation to strengthen us to live the Christian life.

Pray this prayer together:

Holy Spirit, bless me with
Knowledge to know right from wrong;
Courage to stand up and be strong;
Understanding to follow God's way;
Reverence to worship and pray;
Right judgement to enlighten and guide me;
Wisdom to want your presence beside me;
Wonder and Awe to fill me with praise for God and God's creation. Amen.

Wisdom

Wonder and Awe in God's presence

Understanding

Reverence

Right Judgement

Knowledge

Courage

AT HOME

DID YOU KNOW?

Like any gift, the gifts of the Spirit are offered to us and it is up to us to accept and use them.

TIME TOGETHER

Chat Together

Share what you have learned about the gifts of the Holy Spirit with your parent or guardian. See if they have any new or different ideas about how these gifts might help you to live a Christian life.

Respond and Share

Using a wire hanger, make a mobile with the seven gifts of the Holy Spirit. Decide with your parent or guardian where you might hang it up in your home.

Use Your Gifts

Use the gifts of the Holy Spirit to show that you are a Spirit-filled follower of Jesus.

THIS WEEK IN SCHOOL

You are invited to think about:

- Why we celebrate the Sacrament of Confirmation
- What happens during the Rite of Confirmation
- The Confirmation name and sponsor you may choose

KEY WORDS

Sacrament: A sacrament is a special meeting with the Risen Jesus.

Grace: The gift of God's love that helps us to live our lives in the way Jesus showed us. One of the ways grace comes to us is through the sacraments.

Oil of Chrism: The oil that is blessed by the bishop on Holy Thursday and used during the celebration of Baptism and Confirmation.

Veni Creator Spiritus: A Latin phrase meaning 'Come Holy Spirit'.

Confirmation candidate: A person who is celebrating their Confirmation.

Confirmation name: A name chosen by a Confirmation candidate as a sign that they are ready to begin to live in a new way.

Confirmation sponsor: A person chosen by a Confirmation candidate to support him or her in their journey as a follower of Jesus.

THEME 8: THE HOLY SPIRIT | LESSON 3

Come Holy Spirit

THE FAMILY OF THE CHURCH

There are special times in every person's life. For Christians, these times include the celebration of the sacraments. Sacraments are special meetings, or encounters, with the Risen Jesus. We receive the sacraments in order to become closer to God and to the Church. When we celebrate the sacraments, we receive the gift of God's love, which is called **grace**. Grace helps us to grow closer to God and to develop a deeper relationship with him.

Look at the pictures below and see if you can name the seven sacraments of the Church.

THINK ABOUT IT ...

- What are your best memories of your celebration of the sacraments?

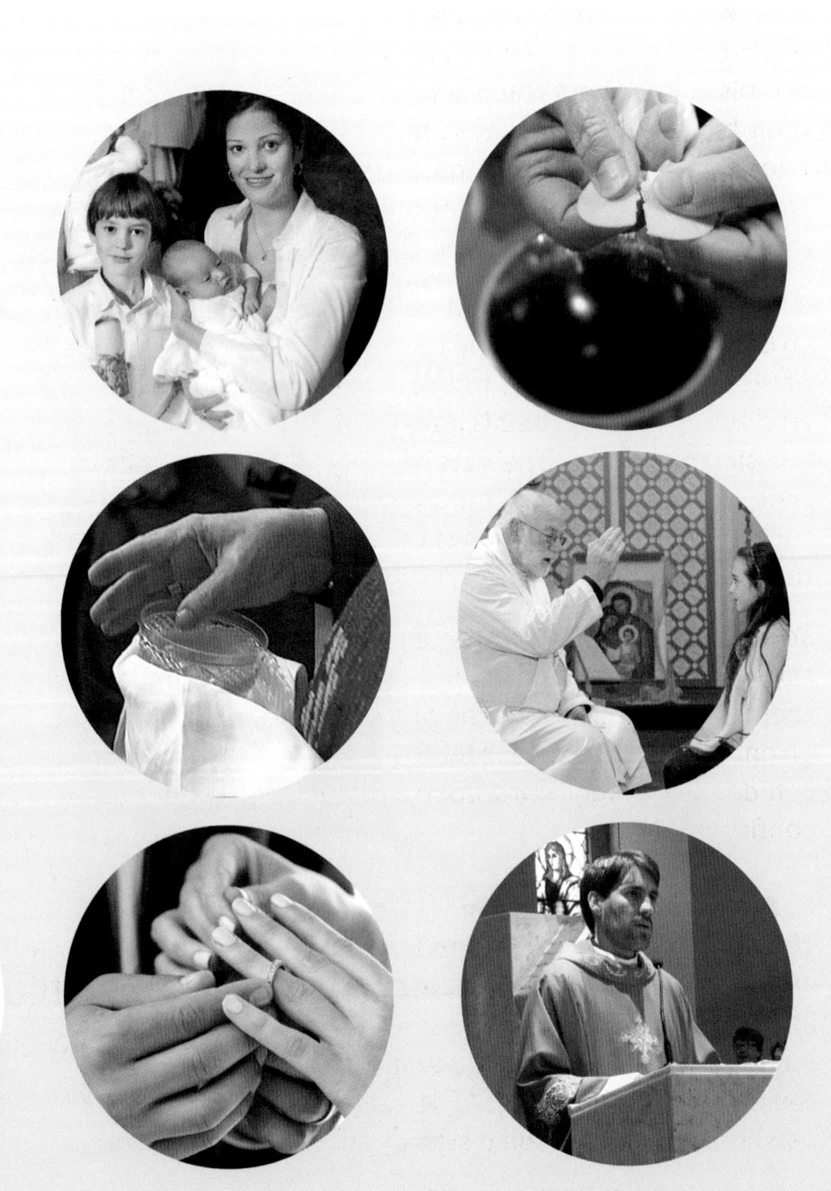

THE RITE OF CONFIRMATION

There are four parts to the Rite of Confirmation. They are:

1. Calling by name

After the Readings and the homily, each of the candidates is called by name and asked to stand. The celebrant gives a short talk about what it means to be confirmed.

2. Renewal of baptismal promises

The candidates are asked to renew their baptismal promises. These are the promises their families made on their behalf when they were baptised. They are now old enough to make these promises themselves. This is their way of saying that they want to confirm the promises made on their behalf at their Baptism.

3. Laying on of hands and calling upon the Holy Spirit

In Old Testament times the laying on of hands was a sign of blessing. The Gospels tell us that, following in this tradition, Jesus placed his hands on people as a sign of blessing or healing. The Acts of the Apostles also tells us that, after Pentecost, Peter and John laid their hands on the newly baptised followers of Jesus, 'and they received the Holy Spirit' (Acts 8:17).

So, too, in Confirmation the celebrant lays his hands upon those whom he is confirming (by extending his hands over them). This is a sign that the gift of the Holy Spirit is being given to them. The celebrant then says a special prayer to call down the Holy Spirit upon those who are about to be confirmed.

4. Anointing with chrism

The candidates go forward to the celebrant to be anointed with the **oil of chrism**. The celebrant dips his right thumb in the chrism and makes the sign of the cross on the forehead of the candidate, saying, '*(Name)*, be sealed with the Gift of the Holy Spirit.' The celebrant then offers the newly confirmed person a sign of peace.

Pope Francis chose his papal name because of his spiritual closeness to St Francis of Assisi

CONFIRMATION NAMES AND CONFIRMATION SPONSORS

For our Baptism, our names and godparents were chosen for us by our families. In Confirmation, candidates accept the responsibility for their own faith, and they choose their own names and sponsors, with guidance from their parents.

Confirmation Names

Names are special and important. Everyone knows us by our name. God knows us by our name. God says to us, 'I have called you by name – you are mine.' People usually choose a new name at Confirmation as a sign that they are ready to try to live in a new way as a follower of Jesus. It is recommended that candidates for Confirmation choose the name of a saint for their Confirmation name, because the saints remind us of how to live our lives as true followers of Jesus.

Confirmation Sponsors

For their child's Baptism, parents, along with other family members, choose godparents who will help them to raise their child to know and love God. In Confirmation, candidates choose for themselves a person who will help them to begin to live a new Christian life, strengthened by the Holy Spirit. It is often a good idea for candidates to ask a godparent to be their Confirmation sponsor, as it is likely that he/she has journeyed with them for most of their lives. In some cases, this is not possible. Candidates can therefore think of someone else who will support their decision to live as a follower of Jesus and as a member of the Church. This person should be a confirmed, practising Catholic, who has received Holy Communion. Except in unusual circumstances, sponsors must not be less than sixteen years old.

FOR MEMORISATION

The seven sacraments of the Church are Baptism, Confirmation, Eucharist, Reconciliation, Anointing of the Sick, Marriage and Holy Orders.

THIS WEEK

The children learned that the sacraments are special meetings, or encounters, with the Risen Jesus. In the Sacrament of Confirmation we confirm the promises made on our behalf at our Baptism. The Sacrament of Confirmation is our opportunity to renew those promises ourselves as followers of Jesus. During the Rite of Confirmation, the celebrant calls on God's Spirit to come upon the candidates for Confirmation. Each candidate is then accompanied by their sponsor to be anointed by the celebrant with the oil of chrism. Each candidate for Confirmation also chooses a new name as a sign that they are ready to live in a new way as a follower of Jesus.

Read the poem 'The Holy Spirit' together.

The Holy Spirit

As glass is soft
and molten in the flame
and moulded by the craftsman's loving hand;
as trees can blow and dance
before the wind
to music piped from where the rushes stand;
as breath gives life
and power to the arm
to pull the oar and raise the haycock high;
the dove of peace
is shielding us from harm;
he hovers in the hearts of you and I.

His fire can warm
and mould me tall and strong.
His wind blows through
my prayer, praise and song.
His Breath fills me with life
so I can be
a sign of love and peace
for all to see.

AT HOME

DID YOU KNOW?

Unlike Eucharist, which we may receive each time we attend Mass, we receive the Sacraments of Baptism and Confirmation only once.

TIME TOGETHER

Chat Together

There is no obligation to celebrate your Confirmation at the end of primary school. Chat about whether or not now is the right time to confirm that you are a member of the Church. It is a big commitment.

Pray Together

Come, Holy Spirit, fill the hearts of your faithful.
Enkindle in us the fire of your love.
Send forth your Spirit and we shall be created,
And you shall renew the face of the earth.

Be Informed

Be sure you know what you are saying 'Yes' to if you decide to celebrate the Sacrament of Confirmation.

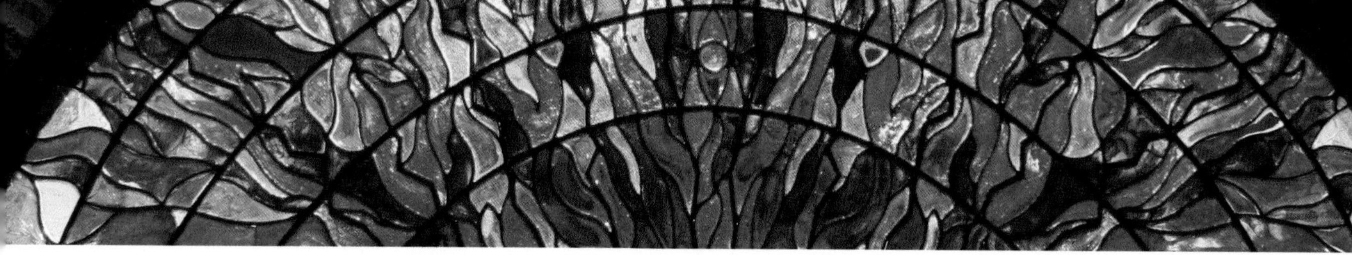

THIS WEEK IN SCHOOL

You are invited to think about:

- How members of the early Christian community lived their lives
- The fruits of the Holy Spirit, and how they can be seen in people's lives
- Whether or not you would like to be confirmed

KEY WORD

Fruits of the Holy Spirit: When the gifts of the Holy Spirit bear fruit in a person's life, we can see the fruits of the Holy Spirit in action in their life.

THEME 8: THE HOLY SPIRIT | LESSON 4

Living a Spirit-Filled Life

PENTECOST AND CONFIRMATION

On the first Pentecost, the Holy Spirit gave the followers of Jesus strength and power like a mighty wind. And, like the wind, it moved them, individually and as a group, to do things that they had never done before – to live in a new way with a new sense of courage and determination, and all because they were filled with the Holy Spirit. In Confirmation, the same Holy Spirit comes to us like a mighty wind, giving us strength and courage to find new and better ways to help bring about the Kingdom of God in our own place and time.

MOVED BY THE SPIRIT

Look at the following notices from shop windows and community noticeboards. In what ways are the people who put them there being moved by the Spirit?

CLOTHES COLLECTION

A collection of clean clothes will be taken up outside Newtown National School this Saturday in support of the work of local priest Fr Kevin Daly, who is now working in Kenya.

Join Us!

The Tidy Towns Committee welcomes new members to help us with our weekly clean-up. Equipment provided!

Can you spare an hour a week?

Help people new to our community to learn English by joining us for a cup of tea and a chat in the parish centre at 10 am on Wednesdays.

THINK ABOUT IT ...

- Can you recall a time when you were moved by the Spirit to do something at home, in school or in your community to help others?

THE FIRST CHRISTIANS

Read this passage from Acts of the Apostles, which describes what happened when the people of Jerusalem heard and believed Peter's message on the first Pentecost.

Life Among the First Christians (Acts 2:41-47)

Many of them believed his message and were baptised, and about three thousand people were added to the group that day. They spent their time in learning from the apostles, taking part in the fellowship, and sharing in the fellowship meals and the prayers.

Many miracles and wonders were being done through the apostles, and everyone was filled with awe. All the believers continued together in close fellowship and shared their belongings with one another. They would sell their property and possessions, and distribute the money among all, according to what each one needed. Day after day they met as a group in the Temple, and they had their meals together in their homes, eating with glad and humble hearts, praising God, and enjoying the good will of all the people. And every day the Lord added to their group those who were being saved.

- What special thing happened to the people who believed Peter's message?
- Can you name some of the things that these believers did from day to day, which showed others that they were followers of Jesus?

JOURNAL EXERCISE

- How would you describe the first Christians – the kind of people they were? Make a list of words that you would use to describe them in your Religious Education journal.

THE FRUITS OF THE HOLY SPIRIT

St Paul wrote a letter to the young Christian community in Galatia, in ancient Turkey. In his letter he said that if we are led or guided by the Spirit, then we will live 'Spirit-filled' lives. St Paul described Spirit-filled lives as lives filled with love, joy, peace, patience, kindness, goodness, gentleness, faithfulness and self-control. These characteristics will be small at first, like seeds, but, if we allow the Holy Spirit to work in us, they will eventually grow to be like fruit on a tree, on display for everyone to see.

THINK ABOUT IT ...

- Which of the fruits of the Holy Spirit can you already see in your life? Which ones would you like to develop further?

FRUITS OF THE HOLY SPIRIT IN ACTION

Read these stories of what happens when people allow the gifts of the Holy Spirit to bear fruit in their lives.

Sister Stanislaus Kennedy (left) and Willie Bermingham (right)

Sister Stanislaus Kennedy, or Sister Stan, as she is known, was born in County Kerry in 1940. At the age of eighteen she felt that God was calling her to a particular way of life, and she decided to become a religious sister. Sr Stan became aware that there were big differences between the lives of those who had enough or plenty of money and the lives of those who lived in poverty. She moved to Dublin in the early 1980s and set about trying to tackle the issue of homelessness. In 1985 she founded the organisation that is now known as Focus Ireland, which helps people in poor circumstances to find and maintain a home. In 1998 Sr Stan also founded The Sanctuary, a meditation centre in Dublin city, where people can find some quiet space in their busy lives.

Willie Bermingham was born in Dublin in 1942. In 1964 he joined Dublin Fire Brigade as a firefighter. Through his work he came across many older people living in awful conditions. Some of them had no heating, others had very little to eat, and many were simply very, very lonely. So, in 1977, Willie founded the organisation called ALONE, whose slogan is 'A Little Offering Never Ends!', to support older people and offer them friendship. Willie died in 1990, but the ALONE organisation is still doing the work that he started. It supports older people who have difficulties with loneliness, social isolation, poor health, poverty, poor housing or homelessness.

FOR MEMORISATION

The Fruits of the Holy Spirit are: love, joy, peace, patience, kindness, goodness, gentleness, faithfulness and self-control.

THINK ABOUT IT ...

- Think about how the fruits of the Holy Spirit can be seen in the lives of the people described above.

THIS WEEK

The children learned that the gifts of the Holy Spirit, given in Baptism, are sealed in those who celebrate the Sacrament of Confirmation. Over time, as we use these gifts in our everyday lives, they 'bear fruit' – we see the good effects that they produce. These fruits, or good effects, which we refer to as the fruits of the Holy Spirit, are: love, joy, peace, patience, kindness, goodness, gentleness, faithfulness and self-control.

Pray this prayer together:

> God our Father,
> may the wind of your Spirit move freely in our hearts
> so that we may bring love, joy and peace
> into the lives of others.
> We ask this through Christ our Lord. Amen.

AT HOME

DID YOU KNOW?

If we look at the lives of Spirit-filled people, we can see the fruits of the Holy Spirit through their actions in the world.

TIME TOGETHER

Chat Together

Talk about something that you or a member of your family did that showed one or more of the fruits of the Holy Spirit in action – perhaps an act of charity, a kind act for a neighbour or friend, or a loving action within your own home.

Record and Share

Describe the action that you have talked about in your Religious Education journal, and mention which of the fruits of the Holy Spirit can be seen in it. Include pictures or photos if you wish. Share your work with your parent or guardian.

Be Fruitful

Each day, try to show the fruits of the Holy Spirit in all the little things you say and do.

THIS WEEK IN SCHOOL

You are invited to think about:

- Your parish community
- The diocese to which your parish belongs
- The most rewarding and challenging aspects of being a bishop

KEY WORDS

Parish: The local Church community and the place in which the Church community is located.

Parish priest: The leader of a parish.

Diocese: An area made up of a number of parishes. There are twenty-six Catholic dioceses in Ireland.

Bishop: A priest who is ordained to be a leader in a diocese.

Servant: In the Bible this word is used for a person who puts himself or herself at the service of another.

Deacons: Men who are ordained to serve the Church, but who are not priests.

Patron: Someone who gives money and other forms of support to an organisation, a person or a cause.

Parish Pastoral Council: A team of people who help to organise the work of the parish.

THEME 9: WE ARE CALLED TO LOVE AND SERVE THE CHURCH | LESSON 1

Exploring Our Diocese

THE PARISH

Our schools and our homes are situated in a **parish**. There are churches, schools, shops, clubs and other facilities in every parish. A **parish priest** or an administrator is in charge of the parish. He organises the events in the life of the parish. He visits the families and helps them with important occasions in their lives, such as Baptisms, marriages and funerals. He usually has a team to help him in this work.

- Can you name the parish that our school is in?
- If you live in a different parish, can you name that parish?
- How many churches are in our parish? Do you know the names of those churches?
- How many priests are in our parish? Do you know their names?
- Do you know anyone else who works with the priest(s) in our parish?

THE DIOCESES OF IRELAND

Every parish in Ireland belongs to a particular **diocese**. Look at the map and answer these questions about the dioceses of Ireland:

- How many Catholic dioceses are there in Ireland?
- Which diocese do we live in?
- Which dioceses border our diocese?
- The dioceses of Ireland are organised into provinces. There are four Church provinces (or ecclesiastical provinces) in Ireland, just like there are four geographical provinces, but these four Church provinces are not called Ulster, Munster, Leinster and Connacht. What are they called?
- Which Church province do we live in?

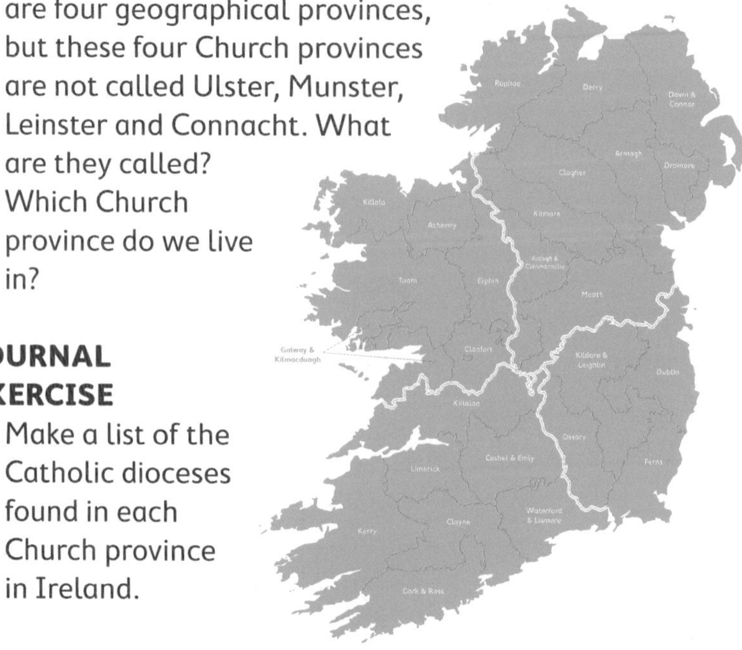

JOURNAL EXERCISE

- Make a list of the Catholic dioceses found in each Church province in Ireland.

Ordination of a bishop

THE BISHOP

Each diocese has a priest who is its leader and chief teacher. This man is called a **bishop**. Bishops continue the work of the twelve apostles in caring for the Church, the People of God. Jesus said about all leaders in the Church: 'The leader must be like the **servant**' (Luke 22:26). The bishop has a lot of responsibilities. For example:

- He appoints priests and **deacons** to the parishes of the diocese.
- He ordains priests and deacons in the Sacrament of Holy Orders.
- He confirms children in the Sacrament of Confirmation, though priests, who are nominated by the bishop to do so, may also administer the Sacrament of Confirmation.
- He is often the **patron** of schools and colleges and has an important role to play in shaping how the faith is taught in the diocese.
- He oversees many diocesan committees that work at helping the local Church to grow and meet the needs of its people.
- He meets with the other bishops in the country to consider and respond to the needs of the Church nationally. This gathering is known as an episcopal conference.
- Every five years the bishop, along with other bishops of the region, travels to Rome. He visits the Pope and submits an important report on his particular diocese.

Bishops wear or carry four particular items:

Pectoral cross: This cross is attached to a long chain so that it can be worn near the heart.

Ring: Just like married people wear rings, the bishop wears a ring to symbolise his relationship with, and love for, the people of his diocese.

Mitre: This is a large headpiece worn by a bishop when he is celebrating Mass or leading another religious service. Underneath he wears a skullcap known as a *zucchetto*.

Crosier: This long stick or staff is also carried by the bishop when he is celebrating Mass or leading another religious service. It represents his role as the shepherd of the diocese.

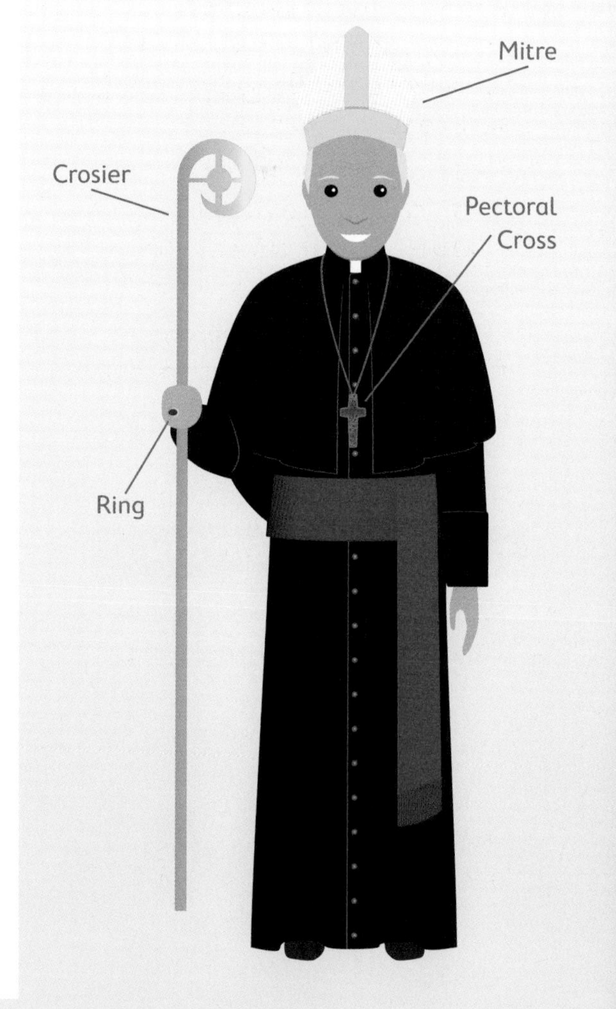

Meet Bishop John Fleming ...

'Hello! My name is Bishop John Fleming. I was born in 1948 and I am the eldest of five children. I grew up on our family farm in Ardpatrick, County Limerick, and went to school in Ardpatrick National School. I then went to secondary school at St Munchin's College, Limerick.

I was ordained a priest on 18 June 1972, having attended St Patrick's College, Maynooth and the Irish College in Rome. I then began to work as a priest in St Michael's Parish, Limerick. Two years later I went back to Rome, and then to London to study further. In 1987 I moved to Rome and began to work at the Irish College, where I had studied.

I was ordained a bishop for the Diocese of Killala in St Muredach's Cathedral in April 2002. St John Paul II was the Pope at the time. As well as my work in the diocese, I also work on behalf of all the bishops at a national level.'

THE WORK OF A DIOCESE

Just as members of a parish community can be involved in many different ways in the life and work of the Church at local level, many people also serve the Church at diocesan level. Some of the activities of a diocese include:

- Looking after the needs of priests, especially priests who are old or ill.
- Helping parishes to look after churches and other properties that belong to the parish.
- Providing help and support to Catholic schools.
- Offering opportunities for young people to attend national and international events, such as World Youth Day.
- Providing training and support for people who work and volunteer in the parish, including on the **Parish Pastoral Council**.
- Offering opportunities for adults to learn more about their faith.

THINK ABOUT IT ...

- From what you have learned about all of the things that happen in the local parish and diocese, what do you find the most interesting, and why?

FOR MEMORISATION

Jesus said, 'The leader must be like the servant.' (Luke 22:26)

THIS WEEK

The children learned that there are twenty-six dioceses in Ireland, which are organised into four provinces. Each diocese is led by a bishop. The children researched their own diocese and they now know the name of their parish, diocese and bishop. They have also learned about some of the work that goes on in the parish and diocese.

Pray this prayer together:

Loving God,
bless all the people who live and work in our diocese.
Bless our priest(s) and bishop(s) who help us to grow in faith and love.
Bless all the people of our parish, that they may continue to know, love and serve God as a parish community.
Help us to see how we can play our part in making our parish a sign of your light in the world.
We ask this through Christ our Lord. Amen.

Christ Giving the Keys to St Peter by Pietro Perugino (1481–1482)

AT HOME

DID YOU KNOW?

The bishops (including the Pope) are successors of the apostles.

TIME TOGETHER

Chat Together
Chat about a time when someone in your family met a bishop. This may have been when someone in the family celebrated their Confirmation. Talk about the occasion.

Respond and Share
If possible, paste a photograph (or draw a picture) of the meeting between someone in your family and a bishop into your Religious Education journal. Write a short description about the meeting. Share your work with your parent or guardian.

Be Involved
Find out how you can become more involved in the work and activities of your parish.

THIS WEEK IN SCHOOL

You are invited to think about:
- Pope Francis' vocation story
- The different things a priest does in the parish community
- How you can respond to God's call to make his love known in the world

KEY WORDS

Seminarian: A man training to be a priest. This usually takes about seven years.

Seminary: Name given to the college where men train to be priests.

Ordination: The ceremony during which a man becomes a deacon, priest or bishop.

Sacrament of Holy Orders: The sacrament through which a man is ordained as a deacon, priest or bishop.

THEME 9: WE ARE CALLED TO LOVE AND SERVE THE CHURCH | LESSON 2

The Sacrament of Holy Orders

RECALL THE STORY: 'JORGE HEARS AND RESPONDS TO GOD'S CALL'

- How old was Jorge when he decided to ask his girlfriend to marry him?
- Where did he go on his way to meet her?
- What did Jorge say about the moment when he realised that he wanted to give all of himself and all of his love to the Church?
- What did Jorge tell his mother he wanted to be?
- What were his favourite hobbies?
- How old was Jorge when he was ordained a priest?
- How old was he when he became the Pope?
- What name did he choose when he became the Pope?

Meet seminarian Thomas Small ...

'Hi! My name is Thomas Small and I am studying to be a priest in St Patrick's College, Maynooth, County Kildare. Before I became a **seminarian**, I spent fifteen years working in the family business of furniture restoration. I grew up in a home where faith and religion were important, but it took me a while to realise that maybe I wanted to be a priest.

Jesus and the Twelve Apostles (c. 1500)

Here in Maynooth, I study and learn more about God, about the Church and about myself. I also spend some time working with people in parishes, hospitals and nursing homes, trying to understand what life as a priest would be like.

In my spare time, I like to listen to music, and I sing in the college choir.'

THINK ABOUT IT...

- God has called Thomas in a very specific way to make God's love known in the world. How might God be calling you to do the same?

WALKING IN THE FOOTSTEPS OF THE APOSTLES

The twelve apostles whom Jesus chose were, in fact, the first leaders in the Church. They were much like our bishops today.

Jesus told the apostles to go and make new members of the Church by baptising people. Jesus said to them, 'I have been given all authority in heaven and on earth. Go, then, to all peoples everywhere and make them my disciples: baptise them in the name of the Father, the Son, and the Holy Spirit, and teach them to obey everything I have commanded you. And I will be with you always, to the end of the age' (Matthew 28:19-20). Today, priests and deacons continue the work of baptising people so that they become members of the Church, or Christians.

Jesus also gave the apostles the power to forgive sins. Priests today forgive sins through the Sacrament of Reconciliation.

The apostles were all present at the Last Supper, when Jesus changed ordinary bread and wine into his own Body and Blood. Jesus said to the apostles, 'Do this in memory of me.' Priests today honour Jesus' request when they celebrate the Eucharist.

Meet Fr Gerry Moore ...

'Hello! My name is Fr Gerry Moore and I am from North County Dublin. All during school I knew exactly what I wanted to do with my life. I never had a moment's doubt. I wanted to be a chef. I wanted to cook food and travel the world. And I did just that. I went to college in Dublin, and then worked in a hotel in County Kerry before moving for two years to work in the United States of America. When I came home I started to work for a hotel in Dublin, and spent five years there.

Finally, I plucked up the courage to explore something that had entered my mind, on and off, for years. I left my job to embark on a totally new voyage of life and faith. I entered the **seminary** and spent seven wonderful years there.

After my **ordination** in July 2003, I served in a number of parishes. I now work in a very busy parish in Dublin along with our deacon. Together we coordinate the parish pastoral council, parish finance committee, altar servers, Baptism and funeral teams, ministers of the Word and of the Eucharist, music ministry groups, and much, much more! There is Mass every day in our parish, and two Masses on Sundays.

Our aim is for the parish to be a place where all feel welcomed, accepted and valued. We want to create an environment where everyone works together for the greater good of every member of the parish.'

REVISION ACTIVITY

- Make a list in your Religious Education journal of all the things a priest does in a parish.

THE SACRAMENT OF HOLY ORDERS

The ceremony during which a man becomes a priest is called an ordination. During his ordination, a man celebrates the **Sacrament of Holy Orders**. Through the Sacrament of Holy Orders the priest is gifted by the Holy Spirit to lead and serve the People of God. The celebrant in the Sacrament of Holy Orders is a bishop. Like Baptism and Confirmation, ordination only happens once in a lifetime. It cannot be repeated.

- What do you think is happening in each of the pictures on this page?

ART ACTIVITY

- Make a 'Thank You' card for the priest(s) and/or deacon(s) of your parish.

FOR MEMORISATION

Jesus said to his apostles, 'Go, then, to all peoples everywhere and make them my disciples: baptise them in the name of the Father, the Son, and the Holy Spirit, and teach them to obey everything I have commanded you. And I will be with you always, to the end of the age.' (Matthew 28:19-20)

AT HOME

THIS WEEK

The children learned that God calls some men to love and serve the Church as priests, just as Jesus called the twelve apostles. Priests show their love for God and for the Church in many ways, such as by baptising people, celebrating Mass, visiting schools, visiting the sick and elderly, and, above all, teaching people about God.

Pray this prayer together:

> God our Father,
> in Baptism you call us to bring your love and your light to the world.
> Today we pray for those whom you call to be your priests.
> May they have the courage to respond to that call,
> and may we support them and pray for them as they fulfil their vocation.
> We make this prayer through Christ, our Lord. Amen.

DID YOU KNOW?

Men are ordained during the Sacrament of Holy Orders.

TIME TOGETHER

Chat Together
Recall any of your family's celebrations that took place in the church. Talk about what made those celebrations special for your family.

Respond and Share
Write in your Religious Education journal about a special occasion that your family celebrated in church. If possible, include a photo or drawing of the occasion. Share your work with your parent or guardian.

Be Thankful
Being a priest is a wonderful vocation, but it is also a challenging one. Think about saying thank you to your local priests for the work they do the next time you see them.

THIS WEEK IN SCHOOL

You are invited to think about:

- What happened at the Last Supper
- The stories in the Bible about other meals that Jesus shared with people
- What happened to the two disciples on the road to Emmaus
- How the Risen Jesus is present with us at Mass

KEY WORDS

Eucharist: The word 'Eucharist' comes from a Greek word meaning 'thanksgiving'. The Eucharist is one of the seven sacraments of the Catholic Church. The word 'Eucharist' is also often used to mean the Mass.

Consecration: Name for the part of the Mass where the bread and wine are changed into the Body and Blood of Jesus Christ. The Consecration takes place during the Eucharistic Prayer.

Transubstantiation: The name for the way ordinary bread and wine, by the power of the Holy Spirit, are changed into the Body and Blood of Jesus Christ at the Consecration of the Mass (Eucharist). After the Consecration,Christ himself is present in a true, real and substantial manner. Jesus Christ continues to be present in the Blessed Sacrament after Mass has ended. When people receive Holy Communion in the Sacrament of the Sick, they receive the consecrated host that has been reserved in the tabernacle.

THEME 10: THE MASS | LESSON 1

On the Road to Emmaus

THE LAST SUPPER

In his first letter to the people of Corinth, St Paul reminded the people about the Last Supper, the last meal that Jesus had with his apostles before he died. The words that Jesus said at that meal, and the actions that he carried out, are repeated at every Mass during the celebration of the **Eucharist**. Here is a passage from St Paul's letter describing what happened at the Last Supper.

1 Corinthians 11:23-25

The Lord Jesus, on the night he was betrayed, took a piece of bread, gave thanks to God, broke it, and said, 'This is my body, which is for you. Do this in memory of me.' In the same way, after the supper he took the cup and said, 'This cup is God's new covenant, sealed with my blood. Whenever you drink it, do so in memory of me.'

JOURNAL EXERCISE

- There are many stories in the Bible of Jesus sharing meals with people. Choose three of the following Scripture references. Look them up and write the verses into your Religious Education journal.

Matthew 9:10 · Mark 2:15 · Matthew 14:19 · Mark 14:3
Luke 22:19 · John 21:12 · Luke 7:36 · Luke 15:2

Now read what happened to two disciples as they walked along the road to Emmaus three days after Jesus was crucified.

The Walk to Emmaus (Luke 24:13-35)

On that same day two of Jesus' followers were going to a village named Emmaus, about seven miles from Jerusalem, and they were talking to each other about all the things that had happened. As they talked and discussed, Jesus himself drew near and walked along with them; they saw him, but somehow did not recognise him. Jesus said to them, 'What are you talking about to each other, as you walk along?'

They stood still, with sad faces. One of them, named Cleopas, asked him, 'Are you the only visitor in Jerusalem who doesn't know the things that have been happening there these last few days?'

'What things?' he asked.

'The things that happened to Jesus of Nazareth,' they answered. 'This man was a prophet and was considered by God and by all the people to be powerful in everything he said and did. Our chief priests and rulers handed him over to be sentenced to death, and he was crucified. And we had hoped that he would be the one who was going to set Israel free! Besides all that, this is now the third day since it happened. Some of the women of our group surprised us; they went at dawn to the tomb, but could not find his body. They came back saying they had seen a vision of angels who told them that he is alive. Some of our group went to the tomb and found it exactly as the women had said, but they did not see him.'

Then Jesus said to them, 'How foolish you are, how slow you are to believe everything the prophets said! Was it not necessary for the Messiah to suffer these things and then to enter his glory?' And Jesus explained to them what was said about himself in all the Scriptures, beginning with the books of Moses and the writings of all the prophets.

As they came near the village to which they were going, Jesus acted as if he were going farther; but they held him back, saying, 'Stay with us; the day is almost over and it is getting dark.' So he went in to stay with them. He sat down to eat with them, took the bread, and said the blessing; then he broke the bread and gave it to them. Then their eyes were opened and they recognised him, but he disappeared from their sight. They said to each other, 'Wasn't it like a fire burning in us when he talked to us on the road and explained the Scriptures to us?'

They got up at once and went back to Jerusalem, where they found the eleven disciples gathered together with the others and saying, 'The Lord is risen indeed! He has appeared to Simon!'

The two then explained to them what had happened on the road, and how they had recognised the Lord when he broke the bread.

The ruins of Emmaus as they appeared to artist Harry Fenn in the 1880s

- Where was the village of Emmaus located?
- What did the Risen Jesus ask the two disciples when he met them?
- What had the disciples hoped, before Jesus died?
- Why did the Risen Jesus say that the disciples were 'foolish'?
- What happened when they arrived at Emmaus?
- When did the disciples recognise the Risen Jesus?
- Where did the disciples go then and what did they do?
- Who else had the Risen Jesus appeared to?

THINK ABOUT IT ...

- The disciples only recognised the Risen Jesus when he shared the meal with them. What other Scripture stories does this remind you of?

FOR MEMORISATION

Then he took a piece of bread, gave thanks to God, broke it, and gave it to them, saying, 'This is my body, which is given for you. Do this in memory of me.' (Luke 22:19)

THE RISEN JESUS COMES TO US, TOO, AT MASS

The Risen Jesus, whom we sometimes call 'Christ', shared a meal with the two disciples whom he met on the road to Emmaus. At Mass, at the **Consecration**, which happens during the Eucharistic Prayer, ordinary bread and wine are changed into the Body and Blood of Jesus Christ through the action of the Holy Spirit. This change is called **transubstantiation**. When we receive Holy Communion at Mass, the Risen Jesus is present with us in a true, real and substantial manner. We can respond to Jesus Christ's presence in others by loving and serving them in the way Jesus showed us.

AT HOME

THIS WEEK

The children recalled stories from the Bible about Jesus sharing meals with people. The most important of these meals was the Last Supper, which Jesus shared with his apostles on the night before he died. The following Sunday, two of Jesus' disciples were walking to a village called Emmaus, about seven miles outside of Jerusalem, when the Risen Jesus joined them, although they did not recognise him at first. It only became clear to the two disciples who the stranger was when he shared a meal with them. The children were reminded that the Risen Jesus is present with us, too, at Mass.

Pray this prayer together:

God our Father,
may the wind of your Spirit move freely in our hearts and in our lives.
May your Spirit move us to live as followers of Jesus
and imitate him in all that we do and say;
to reach out to those in need,
to help those who are poor
and to care for one another. Amen.

The Supper at Emmaus has long been a favourite subject in sacred art, such as this stained-glass window from Antwerp, Belgium

DID YOU KNOW?

During every Mass, ordinary bread and wine are changed into the Body and Blood of Jesus Christ through the action of the Holy Spirit. This change is called transubstantiation.

TIME TOGETHER

Chat Together
Talk about how easy or difficult it is to believe that ordinary bread and wine are changed into the Body and Blood of Jesus Christ at Holy Communion.

Respond and Share
When do the members of your family go to Mass together? Write about those times in your Religious Education journal. Share your work with your parent or guardian.

Be Present
Jesus invites all of us to share a special meal with him and his followers every week. Consider accepting Jesus' invitation.

THIS WEEK IN SCHOOL

You are invited to think about:

- What happens at Mass
- How the four main parts of the Mass reflect the experience of the disciples on the road to Emmaus
- How you can show by your words and actions that you are a follower of Jesus

KEY WORDS

Introductory Rites: The opening part of the Mass.

The Liturgy of the Word: The part of the Mass where we listen to the Word of God, reflect on it, and pray for our needs.

The Liturgy of the Eucharist: The part of the Mass where we thank God for all that we have. The bread and wine are transformed into the Body and Blood of Jesus Christ, which we receive in Holy Communion.

Eucharistic Prayer: The Eucharistic Prayer is at the heart of the Liturgy of the Eucharist. It is a special prayer of thanks addressed to God the Father, which is said by the celebrant (a priest or bishop), who represents Christ, on behalf of all the people.

Consecration: Name for the part of the Mass, during the Eucharistic Prayer, when the bread and wine are changed into the Body and Blood of Jesus Christ.

Concluding Rites: The final part of the Mass.

THEME 10: THE MASS | LESSON 2

The Table of the Lord

EXPERIENCES OF MASS

Read these statements from two children about their experiences of Mass and what it means to them.

'My name is Nicholi. I remember very well the first time I received Holy Communion at Mass. It was three years ago, when I was eight. I felt very special and very important. It was nice to be able to receive Holy Communion with the rest of my family. Up to then, I had just walked up for a blessing. My family didn't always go to Mass, but we made a big effort to go coming up to my First Communion, and we've continued to do so ever since.'

'My name is Aisling. A Mass that is really special for me is my granny's anniversary Mass. My granny died before I was born, so I didn't get to meet her. But every year my aunties, uncles and cousins all go to a Mass to remember her and to pray for her. My grandad comes too, even though he lives in a nursing home now. Afterwards, we go for breakfast at my Aunty Julie's house, and my mam and her sisters and brothers all tell stories about my granny. So I feel like I know her a little bit.'

JOURNAL EXERCISE

- Can you recall a Mass that you took part in that was special for you? Why was it special? Who was there? What thoughts come to your mind when you remember it? Record those memories in your Religious Education journal.

RECALL THE WALK TO EMMAUS

Use the pictures below to help you to remember what happened to the two disciples on the road to Emmaus.

THE MASS

Look at the pictures of the four main parts of the Mass and read about what happens during each of those parts.

1. Introductory Rites

The Mass begins when the People of God gather together. We gather as a community of believers to praise God and to bring our needs before him. When the priest, who leads the Mass, comes to the altar, he reminds us of why we are there when he says these words: 'In the name of the Father, and of the Son, and of the Holy Spirit.' We respond by saying 'Amen'.

Then we say sorry to God and to others for anything that we have done wrong. This is called the *Penitential Act*. We pray the *Confiteor* as part of the Penitential Act. The *Lord, Have Mercy* prayer follows. Finally, in the *Gloria*, we give praise for all that God is and for all that God does.

2. The Liturgy of the Word

During this part of the Mass we listen to the Readings. The First Reading is usually from the Old Testament. The Second Reading is from the New Testament. The final reading is from the Gospel. These are not just stories *about* God from the Bible. These words *are* the Word of God.

3. The Liturgy of the Eucharist

This is the part of the Mass where, in the **Eucharistic Prayer**, which the priest says on behalf of the people, we thank God for all that we have and for all that God has done for us. We thank God especially for giving us the gift of his Son, Jesus.

The Eucharistic Prayer is at the heart of the Liturgy of the Eucharist. As the priest prays this prayer, we remember the words and actions of Jesus at the Last Supper, when he took bread and wine, shared them, and said, 'Do this in memory of me.'

4

During the Eucharistic Prayer, the bread and wine are changed into the Body and Blood of Christ by the power of the Holy Spirit. We call this the **Consecration**.

The **Communion Rite** is the final part of the Liturgy of the Eucharist, during which we receive Holy Communion and welcome the Risen Jesus into our hearts and into our lives.

4. Concluding Rites

At the end of the Mass the priest gives the final blessing and invites us to go and show by our lives that we are followers of Jesus. We need the help of the Holy Spirit to live in this way.

THINK ABOUT IT ...

- What do you notice about the four main parts of the Mass when you look at them against the pictures on page 110 that illustrate the story 'The Walk to Emmaus'?

THE STORY CONTINUES TODAY

The story of the disciples on the road to Emmaus did not finish when the two disciples went back to Jerusalem to tell the others about what they had seen and heard. Those disciples and others renewed their efforts to live as followers of Jesus and helped to build up the early Christian Church. If our participation in the Mass is really to be like what the disciples experienced on their journey to Emmaus, then we, too, should leave Mass ready to show by our words and actions that we are followers of Jesus.

FOR MEMORISATION

The four parts of the Mass:

- Introductory Rites
- The Liturgy of the Word
- The Liturgy of the Eucharist
- Concluding Rites

AT HOME

THIS WEEK

The children learned about how the structure of the Mass is mirrored in the experience that the disciples had on the road to Emmaus: the followers of Jesus gather together, listen to the Word of God from the Scriptures, share a meal where the Risen Jesus is truly present, and then go to love God and others in their ordinary lives. If our participation in the Mass is really to be like what the disciples experienced on their journey to Emmaus, then we, too, should leave Mass ready to show by our words and actions that we are followers of Jesus.

Chat together about how the people in these pictures are living as followers of Jesus. Then talk about the ways in which you can show by your words and actions that you are followers of Jesus.

DID YOU KNOW?

Just as their meeting with the Risen Jesus on the road to Emmaus strengthened the faith of the two disciples, our taking part in the Mass can also give us the strength to love and serve God in a more real and determined way.

TIME TOGETHER

Respond and Share

Write or draw a picture about a time when someone in your family did an act of kindness or love – something that followers of Jesus would do. Share your work with your parent or guardian.

Pray Together

Holy, holy, holy Lord God of hosts.
Heaven and earth are full of your glory.
Hosanna in the highest.
Blessed is he who comes in the name of the Lord.
Hosanna in the highest.

Be Like Jesus

Jesus Christ's presence in you can help you to love and serve others. Try to act as Jesus would, especially when you see people who are in need.

THIS WEEK IN SCHOOL

You are invited to think about:

- What Catholics believe about death, heaven and eternal life
- Why we celebrate the Feast of All Saints and the Feast of All Souls
- How Jews and Muslims show respect for the dead

KEY WORDS

Saint: A person who, after living a good life by loving God and others, dies in the state of grace and is now in heaven. The saints are role models for us today.

Feast of All Saints: 1 November, a day when we honour all the saints, including those who have not been canonised. This feast is also known as All Saints' Day or the Solemnity of All Saints.

Feast of All Souls: 2 November, a day when we remember and pray for all those who have died. This feast is also known as All Souls' Day or the Commemoration of All the Faithful Departed.

Traditions: Customs and practices that have been in existence for a long time, and that are usually passed from one generation to the next.

Shiva: A week of mourning observed by Jews when a close family member dies.

Memorial: Meaning 'in memory of'. This word is often used to refer to a symbol or ritual in memory of someone who has died.

(SEASONAL/ADDITIONAL) LESSON 1

Death and Eternal Life

RECALL THE STORY: 'CLIONA AND THE SEA STONE'

- What gave Cliona the idea that there was something going on at home?
- Where did Cliona go when she discovered that there was something wrong with Gran?
- What explanation did Gran give Cliona about where she was going and what was going to happen there?
- Did Gran think she was going to die soon?
- What did Gran say about what would happen when she would eventually die?
- How did Gran think the sea stone would help Cliona in the future?

THINK ABOUT IT ...

- What do you think it would be like to live in happiness and love with God forever in heaven?

ACTIVITY

- Record an image of heaven as you imagine it to be, using words, colour, symbols and/or drawings.

LIFE AFTER DEATH

You may recall learning in Third Class/Primary 5 about how Jesus used the image of 'many rooms in my Father's house' to speak of heaven. Jesus said:

'There are many rooms in my Father's house, and I am going to prepare a place for you. I would not tell you this if it were not so. And after I go and prepare a place for you, I will come back and take you to myself, so that you will be where I am. You know the way that leads to the place where I am going.' (John 14:2-4)

St Brigid

You may also remember from Fourth class/Primary 6 St Paul's image of heaven as like meeting God face to face. St Paul said:

What we see now is like a dim image in a mirror; then we shall see face to face. What I know now is only partial; then it will be complete – as complete as God's knowledge of me. (1 Corinthians 13:12)

St Patrick

After Jesus returned to his Father in heaven, St Paul helped the followers of Jesus to understand what Jesus wanted them to believe about life after death. St Paul said:

Our friends, we want you to know the truth about those who have died, so that you will not be sad, as are those who have no hope. We believe that Jesus died and rose again, and so we believe that God will take back with Jesus those who have died believing in him. (1 Thessalonians 4:13-14)

St Thérèse of Lisieux

THE SAINTS

The **saints** were not perfect men and women. They were ordinary people like us! They felt all the ordinary feelings that we feel: happy and sad, angry and jealous, guilty and disappointed. They were just ordinary people who did extraordinary things in their lives because they loved God and their neighbour as Jesus asked them to. We can ask the saints to pray for us and to guide us so that we, too, can become saints.

JOURNAL EXERCISE

- Write a short account in your Religious Education journal about a saint whom you admire, and say what you admire about them. You might like to draw a picture or symbols to accompany your description.

WE HONOUR THE SAINTS AND ALL THOSE WHO HAVE DIED

The Church sets aside the full month of November as a special month to remember and pray for all those who have died.

Catholics celebrate the **Feast of All Saints**, or All Saints' Day, on 1 November each year. On this day we honour all saints, including our family and friends who lived lives of love but who may not have been canonised, and who are now with God in heaven. We believe that the saints and all those who have died guide and help us on our journey through life. We ask them to pray for us and to help us to live good lives.

Catholics celebrate the **Feast of All Souls**, or All Souls' Day, on 2 November. On that day we remember and pray for all those who have died. Many parishes have special Masses to remember parishioners who have died. Some parishes will also have prayers in the local graveyards. One of the ways we honour the dead is by taking care of their graves.

THINK ABOUT IT ...

- Why do people bring flowers, candles, statues and other items to graves? Does your family have any traditions about visiting the graves of your own family members?

TRADITIONS ASSOCIATED WITH DEATH IN OTHER RELIGIONS

Different religious have different **traditions** and customs to show their respect for their dead. You already know a lot about the Jewish and Islamic faiths. Now you can learn about how Jews and Muslims respect and remember their dead.

Jewish Traditions Around Death

When a close relative of a Jewish person dies, that person enters a week of mourning known as **Shiva**. Those who are in mourning usually stay in the home of the person who has died and do not work for the seven-day Shiva period. Mourners also usually wear a torn black ribbon on their clothing, as a symbol of their broken heart. A tall candle is sometimes burned in the Shiva home as a sign of **memorial**. Jews also have special prayers to mark the passing of loved ones and to celebrate their life.

Islamic Traditions Around Death

When a Muslim dies, they are buried within two days. The body is carried to the graveyard by four men. A procession of friends and relatives follows. After the burial, those who attended the funeral usually go back to the house of the family for a meal. The family then observes a mourning period of forty days. During this time, female family members wear only black. When a woman's husband dies, she wears black for a full year.

FOR MEMORISATION

Eternal rest grant unto them,
O Lord,
and let perpetual light shine
upon them.

THIS WEEK

The children learned that death is a part of every person's life. But Christians believe that God has promised eternal life in heaven to all those who love God and their neighbour. The Catholic Church encourages a deep respect for the dead by celebrating All Saints' Day on 1 November and All Souls' Day on 2 November. The children have also learned about some of the Jewish and Islamic traditions around death.

Pray the poem 'All Saints, All Souls' together.

All Saints, All Souls
Remember those
Who kept the faith
Who always turned to pray,
Who showed the love of Jesus
In their lives from day to day.

Remember those
This special time
Who live with God above,
All Saints, All Souls,
And all our own
Who live with God in love.

AT HOME

DID YOU KNOW?

We can ask the saints and all those who have died to guide us on our journey through life.

TIME TOGETHER

Chat Together
Think about the different ways in which your family pray for, respect and remember your own loved ones who have died.

Respond and Share
In your Religious Education journal, write about how your family prays for, respects and remembers one person in particular. Include a photo or drawing of that person. Share your work with your parent or guardian.

Remember and Pray
We remember our dead in a special way in November. This November, pray for all the people you know who have died.

THIS WEEK IN SCHOOL

You are invited to think about:

- When and how you take time out for quiet reflection
- How Jesus resisted temptation
- How you can answer the call to pray, abstain from some of the things you like, and do good during Lent

KEY WORDS

Tempt: Try to get someone to do something wrong by offering them a bribe or something you know they might like.

Temptation: A strong attraction towards something that we know is wrong.

Devils: The name given to fallen angels who were created good but who turned away from God and did evil things. Satan was the devil who tempted Jesus.

Repent: To be sorry for our wrongdoing and to seek God's forgiveness.

Abstain: To abstain from something is to choose not to do something, especially something that we like to do. The Church asks us to abstain from some of the things we like during Lent. This usually requires self-control and a willingness to make sacrifices.

Fast: Go without food for a period of time. The Church asks adults to fast on Ash Wednesday by eating only one full meal and two smaller ones as an expression of sorrow for their wrongdoings, and as a way of following the example of Jesus, who fasted for forty days in the desert.

(SEASONAL/ADDITIONAL) LESSON 2

Lent: A Time for Reflection

WE ALL NEED QUIET TIMES

We all need time out from our busy lives just to think and reflect – to get in touch with how we are really feeling deep inside; to reflect on whether we are living in the way Jesus asked us to live; to think about our relationship with God and with others; to hear God's voice in our hearts; and to really get to know ourselves.

When we want to reflect and pray, it can be easier to do so in a quiet place, where there are no distractions. Finding a quiet time and space can be difficult in today's world of mobile phones and fast living.

THINK ABOUT IT ...

- Look at these images. Which place would you like to go to if you wanted to spend some quiet time alone with your thoughts?

JESUS IN THE DESERT

Just like us, Jesus needed and sought out quiet spaces where he could reflect and pray and get in touch with his innermost thoughts. St Luke tells us the story of what happened when Jesus went into the desert after John had baptised him in the River Jordan.

The Temptation of Jesus (Luke 4:1-13)

Jesus returned from the Jordan full of the Holy Spirit and was led by the Spirit into the desert, where he was **tempted** by the **Devil** for forty days. In all that time he ate nothing, so that he was hungry when it was over.

The Devil said to him, 'If you are God's Son, order this stone to turn into bread.'

But Jesus answered, 'The scripture says, "Human beings cannot live on bread alone." '

Then the Devil took him up and showed him in a second all the kingdoms of the world. 'I will give you all this power and all this wealth,' the Devil told him. 'It has all been handed over to me, and I can give it to anyone I choose. All this will be yours, then, if you worship me.'

Jesus answered, 'The scripture says, "Worship the Lord your God and serve only him!" '

Then the Devil took him to Jerusalem and set him on the highest point of the Temple, and said to him, 'If you are God's Son, throw yourself down from here. For the scripture says, "God will order his angels to take good care of you." It also says, "They will hold you up with their hands so that not even your feet will be hurt on the stones." '

But Jesus answered, 'The scripture says, "Do not put the Lord your God to the test." '

When the Devil finished tempting Jesus in every way, he left him for a while.

- How long did Jesus stay in the desert?
- What was the first thing the Devil tempted Jesus to do? And how did Jesus respond?
- What was the second thing the Devil tempted Jesus to do? And how did Jesus respond to this?
- What was the final thing the Devil tempted Jesus to do? And what was Jesus' response?
- What did the Devil do when he realised that he was having no success with tempting Jesus?

THINK ABOUT IT ...

- What sort of things are people tempted with today? What kinds of things do you think tempt children of your age?

THE GOODNESS IN US

God sees the goodness that is in each one of us, even when others might not see that goodness or even when we don't see it ourselves. God sees into our heart. God knows us inside out.

But sometimes we don't live up to the goodness that is in us. Sometimes we do or say things that block our goodness. But God is always ready to forgive us when we **repent**, or say sorry, and ask for forgiveness. In the Sacrament of Reconciliation we tell God, through the priest, that we are sorry for the times when we did not live up to the goodness in us. The priest tells us that our sins are forgiven. And then we go out and try again to live as Jesus asked us to.

THINK ABOUT IT ...

- Luke's Gospel tells us that the Holy Spirit led Jesus into the desert. Do you think the Holy Spirit might have helped Jesus when he was being tested by the Devil? How might the Holy Spirit help you when you don't feel like living up to the goodness that is in you?

ACTIVITY

- Design an emoji for the Holy Spirit, which will be a reminder to you that the Holy Spirit is always there to help and guide you.

LENT

During the season of Lent we remember the times when we didn't live up to the goodness that is in us. We tell God that we are sorry and we try again. Lent mirrors the time Jesus spent in the desert. Lent begins on Ash Wednesday. On that day, Christians wear ashes on their forehead as a sign that we admit our failings and that we want to try again to live up to the goodness that we know is within us.

The Church asks all of us to do three things during Lent: to pray, to **abstain** from some of the things we like, and to give to others. The Church asks adults to **fast** on Ash Wednesday by eating only one full meal and two smaller ones.

ACTIVITY

- On a sheet of paper, write a **prayer of petition** or a prayer asking God for forgiveness. This will be a prayer that you can pray throughout the season of Lent.

FOR MEMORISATION

The Catholic Church asks us to do three things during Lent: to pray, to abstain from some of the things we like, and to give to others.

KEY WORD

Prayer of Petition: A prayer in which you ask God for something for yourself.

AT HOME

THIS WEEK

The children heard the story of how Jesus spent forty days in the desert, praying and fasting. During that time, Jesus was tempted by the Devil – with the promise of food, power and wealth – but he resisted the **temptation**. The season of Lent mirrors the time Jesus spent in the desert. During the season of Lent we, too, try to resist temptation. The Church asks all of us to do three things during Lent: to pray, to abstain from some of the things we like, and to give to others. In addition, the Church asks adults to fast on Ash Wednesday by eating only one full meal and two smaller ones as an expression of sorrow for their wrongdoings.

Pray this prayer together:

> The Sprit led Jesus into the desert
> so that he could be closer to God the Father.
> May the same Spirit of God help us
> to live up to the goodness that God sees in each of us.
> May the Spirit of God be with us
> today and every day of our lives. Amen.

DID YOU KNOW?

Lent starts on Ash Wednesday.

TIME TOGETHER

Chat Together
We often only associate Lent with giving something up. Chat about how you might 'give to others' this Lent instead.

Respond and Share
In your Religious Education journal, write about three things that your family might try to do this Lent that would benefit or help others. Share what you have written with your parent or guardian.

Be Selfless
Try your best to show your goodness by being particularly thoughtful and selfless during Lent.

Some medieval monks chose to live in the desert, where they could more easily reflect and pray

THIS WEEK IN SCHOOL

You are invited to think about:

- How different traditions and cultures enrich our lives
- The traditions in your family
- The traditions surrounding St Patrick
- What a pilgrim does when visiting Lough Derg

KEY WORDS

Traditions: Customs and practices that have been in existence for a long time, and that are usually passed from one generation to the next.

Heritage: Something that has been handed on to us from the past.

Culture: Refers to the various aspects of our everyday lives and behaviour that shape who we are and give us our identity as a people. Our culture is influenced by our values, beliefs, traditions and customs.

Cultural Heritage: An expression of the ways of living developed by a community and passed on from generation to generation. Cultural heritage includes customs, practices, places, objects, artistic expressions and values.

Vigil: A period of staying awake when you would normally be asleep, in order to keep watch or pray.

(SEASONAL/ADDITIONAL) LESSON 3

Remembering St Patrick

RECALL THE STORY: 'CHINESE AND IRISH TRADITIONS MEET!'

- Why did Simon's mother call? What did she want to know?
- Why did Yan Yan say that the boys should each get two names?
- What occasion were Yan Yan parents looking forward to celebrating?
- What other event was to be celebrated on the same day?
- What problem arose in relation to the two events?
- What solution did they come up with?

THINK ABOUT IT ...

- What **traditions** does your family have around special days like birthdays, Christmas, Easter, Halloween, etc?

JOURNAL EXERCISE

- Choose three words to describe what is best about your family/the people you live with. Write those words on a clean page of your Religious Education journal, leaving some space between each one. Then, without thinking too much, doodle around the words you have written.

TRADITION AND HERITAGE CONTRIBUTE TO OUR IDENTITY

Just like Yan Yan's and Simon's family, each of our families has its own traditions and family **heritage**. We have different ways of celebrating the events that are important to us. If our family has come from a different country, they will have brought with them some of the **culture** and traditions from that country – their **cultural heritage** – to mix in with the new traditions and customs that they will learn here.

We also live in communities that have their own local heritage. For example, there might be a building, castle, park, well or tower in your community that gives it its unique identity.

The school we attend also has its own heritage – it was founded in a particular time and within a particular tradition. The religious community we belong to has its own heritage too.

All of these different and overlapping traditions exist within our national heritage – the Irish heritage. And they all contribute to making us who we are.

CHRISTIAN CELTIC HERITAGE

Look at the pictures on this page of Irish saints whom you have learned about in previous *Grow in Love* programmes. What do you remember about them?

RECALL THE STORY: 'ST PATRICK AND KING LAOGHAIRE'

- What did God ask St Patrick to do?
- Who were the leaders in Ireland during Celtic times?
- What was the Celtic festival that marked the beginning of summer?
- Who always lit the fire on the Hill of Tara?
- Why did St Patrick light a fire on the Hill of Slane?
- What impressed King Laoghaire so much that he converted to Christianity?
- What symbol of the Trinity did St Patrick use to teach people about God?

JOURNAL EXERCISE

- How do you imagine St Patrick would feel about how St Patrick's Day is celebrated in Ireland now? What do you think he would like about it? What do you think he wouldn't like about it? Write a paragraph on this in your Religious Education journal.

Read this account of a pilgrimage that is associated with St Patrick.

St Patrick's Purgatory

St Patrick's Purgatory is an ancient pilgrimage site on Station Island in Lough Derg, County Donegal. The site dates from the fifth century, when, according to legend, Christ showed St Patrick a cave on Station Island that was supposed to be an entrance to Purgatory, the place where some people who have died spend time before they are ready to enter heaven.

People have gone on pilgrimage to Lough Derg for centuries. The three-day pilgrimage follows the tradition of St Patrick by walking the path that he would have walked. The pilgrimage involves prayer, fasting (one very simple meal each day), walking barefoot, and a twenty-four-hour **vigil**.

Without shoes and sleep and little food, the pilgrims focus instead on what is really important in life, and they often discover their hidden strengths and rediscover the things and people that really matter to them. The pilgrimage to Lough Derg is also a way to remember and honour St Patrick today.

- Where is St Patrick's Purgatory? How did it get its name?
- How long does the pilgrimage last and what do the pilgrims do at Lough Derg?
- What benefits do people get from this pilgrimage?

THINK ABOUT IT ...

- Do you think you would like to visit Lough Derg? Why or why not?

JOURNAL EXERCISE

- Imagine that you have been to Lough Derg. In your Religious Education journal, write a blog telling your friends what it was like.

ST PATRICK'S BREASTPLATE

In ancient times, the breastplate was a central part of the Roman soldier's armour – it provided protection for the torso, the part of the body that contains vital organs like the heart and lungs. With a sturdy breastplate, the soldier would be much less likely to suffer injury or death.

St Patrick once wrote a famous prayer called *St Patrick's Breastplate*, which called on Christ for protection. The words of this prayer are in the opposite column.

FOR MEMORISATION

St Patrick's Breastplate
Christ be with me,
Christ be beside me,
Christ be before me,
Christ be behind me,
Christ be at my right hand,
Christ be at my left hand,
Christ be with me wherever I go,
Christ be my friend, for ever and ever.
Amen.

THIS WEEK

The children learned that there are many different cultures and traditions in modern Ireland and that they all add to the richness of our lives. They recalled that there are many saints associated with Ireland. This week we focused on St Patrick, whose feast day is on 17 March. The children heard the story of St Patrick's association with Lough Derg, and they learned about the ancient traditions that pilgrims participate in when they visit the island.

Read *St Patrick's Breastplate* together.

St Patrick's Breastplate

Christ be with me,
Christ be beside me,
Christ be before me,
Christ be behind me,
Christ be at my right hand,
Christ be at my left hand,
Christ be with me wherever I go,
Christ be my friend, for ever and ever. Amen.

DID YOU KNOW?

Pilgrims have been travelling to Lough Derg in County Donegal since the fifth century.

TIME TOGETHER

Chat Together

Chat about St Patrick's Day and what it represents. Share with your parent or guardian what you have learned about St Patrick.

Respond and Share

In your Religious Education journal, write about how your family celebrates St Patrick's Day. If possible, include a photo or drawing. Share your work with your parent or guardian.

Be Aware

Each of us has our own family traditions, based on our cultural heritage. Chat to members of your family about the traditions you have, and where they came from.

THIS WEEK IN SCHOOL

You are invited to think about:

- What you already know about Mary, the mother of Jesus
- The story of St Luke and the icon of the Black Madonna
- How the phrase 'Hail Mary' is said in different languages

KEY WORDS

Pilgrimage: A journey to a holy place. A pilgrimage is undertaken for various reasons: to seek divine assistance, to show love of God, to do penance or to give thanks.

Marian pilgrimage: A pilgrimage to a holy place devoted to the Blessed Virgin Mary.

Icon: The word 'icon' comes from the Greek word for 'image'. Icons are sacred images that draw the viewer in and hold their attention. An icon usually has no frame and it is normally done on wood. The study of icons is called iconography, and the people who make the icons are called iconographers.

Marian devotions: Traditions, prayers and rituals that honour Mary. The *Rosary* is a prayer that is central to all Marian devotions across the world.

(SEASONAL/ADDITIONAL) LESSON 4

Mary, Mother of Jesus

TEST YOUR MEMORY!

You have learned a lot about Mary, Jesus' mother, from previous *Grow in Love* programmes. Work in pairs or in teams to make a list of ten questions about Mary that you can ask the rest of your classmates. Then you can test them to see how much they know! Sample question: What town did Mary live in?

IMAGES OF MARY

Look at these images of Mary associated with Guadalupe in Mexico, Lourdes in France and Knock in Ireland. These are all places that people go to on **Marian pilgrimages**.

- What do you remember about each of the stories associated with these places?

HAIL MARY

The prayer we most often associate with Mary is the *Hail Mary.* The words 'Hail Mary' mean 'Greetings, Mary'. This is how you would say these words in Spanish, French and Irish:

Spanish: *Dios te salve, Maria*
French: *Je vous salut, Marie*
Irish: *Sé do bheatha, a Mhuire*

ICONS

Throughout the centuries, artists have helped spread the message of Christianity. One special art form, the **icon**, became popular in Eastern Europe and Russia. The word 'icon' comes from the Greek word for 'image'. Icons are said to be written rather than painted. The study of icons is called iconography. An icon usually has no frame and is normally done on wood. Icon artists, known as iconographers, follow particular rules when making an icon.

An icon always has a layer of gold-leaf painted on it. The gold represents the presence of God as light. Icons are only made after much prayer, reflection and meditation. Iconographers never sign their work because they believe they are really working in co-operation with the Holy Spirit.

Although most icons are of figures looking straight out, they are not portraits in the normal sense. Usually, we, the viewers, look at a painting to see what is happening in it. With an icon, it is as if the eyes of the figure are gazing at us. That is why an icon 'holds' our attention. We need to sit and gaze at an icon in silence to 'hear' in our hearts what it is saying to us.

RECALL THE STORY: 'ST LUKE AND THE ICON OF THE BLACK MADONNA'

- Why do you think St Luke wanted to paint Mary?
- What did Mary tell St Luke about Jesus while he was painting?
- Why was Mary surprised by the finished icon? What had she expected?
- What was the neighbours' reaction to the icon?
- When asked by the neighbours how he managed to capture Mary's image so well, St Luke explained: 'I prayed as I painted … and my hands just did the rest.' What do you think he meant by that? Who might have been helping/inspiring him?

THE BLACK MADONNA

The icon of the Black Madonna has been in the care of the Pauline Fathers in Czestochowa, Poland for over six hundred years. The church where the icon is housed has been a place of **pilgrimage** down through the centuries and it continues to attract millions of pilgrims from all around the world. To this day, many people believe that the icon has protected the Polish people.

The Madonna in the icon is often called the 'Queen of Poland', 'Protector of Poland' and 'Our Lady of Czestochowa'. Her feast day is celebrated on 26 August.

The words for 'Hail Mary' in Polish are: *Zdrowas Mario.*

FOR MEMORISATION

Different ways to say 'Hail Mary'
Spanish: Dios te salve, Maria
French: Je vous salut, Marie
Irish: Sé do bheatha, a Mhuire
Polish: Zdrowas Mario

IMAGES OF MARY FROM AROUND THE WORLD

So far, you have learned about Marian shrines in Ireland, France, Mexico and Poland. Many other places and cultures also have traditions and devotions associated with Mary. Here are some more images of Mary from around the world.

La Macarena Filipina, Philippines

Black Madonna of Montserrat, Spain

Immaculate Conception, Bolivia

AT HOME

THIS WEEK

The children learned that members of the Catholic Church around the world have a deep and enduring devotion to Mary, the Mother of God and our Mother. Over the centuries, artists and sculptors have made many wonderful images of Mary. The children heard the legend relating to the icon of the Black Madonna, in Czestochowa, Poland, and they examined an image of the icon. The Madonna in this icon is often called the 'Queen of Poland', 'Protector of Poland' and 'Our Lady of Czestochowa'. The children also looked at other images of Mary from around the world. The Marian shrines in Knock, Lourdes, Guadalupe and Czestochowa are sacred spaces where pilgrims from around the world gather to pray and honour Mary.

Pray the *Hail Mary* together.

Hail Mary

Hail Mary, full of grace,
the Lord is with thee.
Blessed art thou among women
and blessed is the fruit of thy womb, Jesus.
Holy Mary, Mother of God,
pray for us sinners,
now and at the hour of our death. Amen.

Crowds honouring the Black Madonna in Czestochowa, Poland

DID YOU KNOW?

The colour on the face of the icon of Our Lady of Czestochowa has deepened and blackened over time due to lack of light and because of smoke damage from the candles burned in her honour. This is why she is commonly known as the Black Madonna.

TIME TOGETHER

Chat Together

Chat about the different Marian devotions your family may engage in. Is there a picture or icon of Mary in your home? Has anyone in your family ever been to a Marian shrine? Do you reflect or pray when you hear the Angelus bells?

Respond and Share

Write about one way in which your family honours Mary, or, if you don't have such a tradition, one way in which you could start to honour Mary this May. Share your work with your parent or guardian.

Be Grace-filled

In the first line of the *Hail Mary*, we say that Our Lady is 'full of grace' – full of God's love. You can pray to Mary that you, too, may be filled with the love of God, and that you may be ready to share that love in your daily life.

THIS WEEK IN SCHOOL

You are invited to think about:

- The Jewish festivals of Rosh Hashanah, Yom Kippur and Sukkot
- The importance of these festivals for Jewish families

KEY WORDS

Rosh Hashanah: Festival to celebrate the beginning of the Jewish New Year.

Yom Kippur: This day of repentance is the holiest day of the year for Jews. It is also known as the Day of Atonement.

Sukkot: Jewish festival, also known as the Feast of Tabernacles.

Bar Mitzvah/Bat Mitzvah: Ceremony at which a Jewish boy or girl becomes a 'Son/Daughter of the Commandment'. This means that they are now old enough to keep the commandments that are set out in the Torah.

Sukkah: A special tent-like structure usually built in the back garden of Jewish homes each year during the festival of Sukkot to remind the family of the tents or huts in which the Israelites lived when they were wandering in the desert for forty years.

(SEASONAL/ADDITIONAL) LESSON 5: JUDAISM (I)

Rosh Hashanah, Yom Kippur and Sukkot

TEST YOUR MEMORY!

You have already learned a lot about the Jewish faith in previous *Grow in Love* programmes. Try to answer these questions to test your memory!

- What is the name of the Jewish day of worship?
- What sacred book of the Jews contains the first five books of the Old Testament?
- Where do Jews gather to pray?
- Who leads the people in prayer?
- What is the name of the place in the synagogue where Jews keep their holiest scrolls?
- What is the name of the skullcap worn by Jewish men and boys?
- What is the *Shema*?
- What is a mezuzah?
- What is a tallit?
- What is the Kiddush?

Bar Mitzvah celebration in Jerusalem

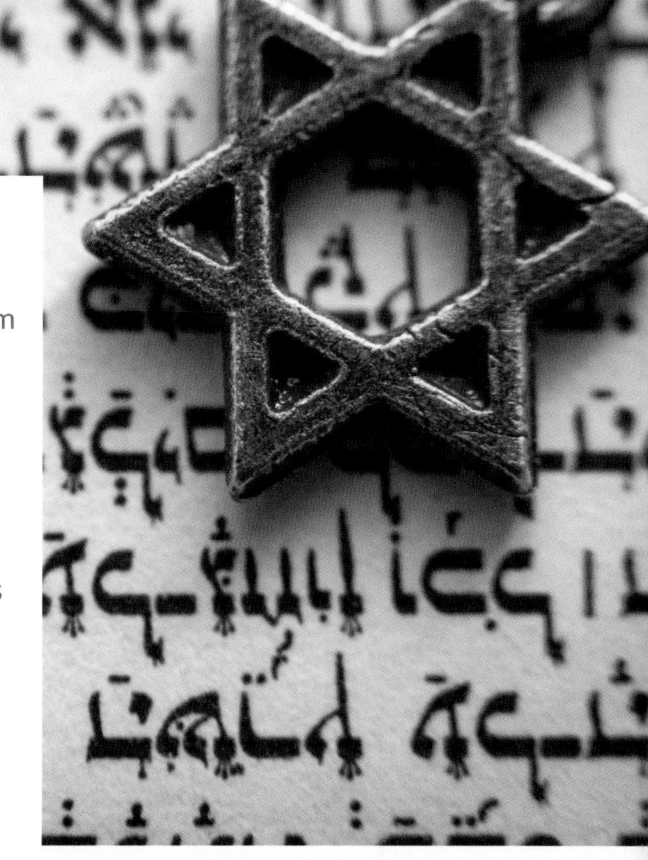

FACT FILE: JUDAISM

- There are approximately fourteen million Jewish people in the world today.
- The Jewish people are descendants of Abraham, whom God chose to lead his people out of slavery in Egypt. Jews honour Abraham as their Father in Faith.
- Jewish people call God Yahweh.
- The Sacred Scriptures of the Jewish people are called the Tanakh. The Tanakh contains the Torah, which is made up of the first five books of the Old Testament, the books of the prophets, and a collection of writings about the history of the Jewish people, called the Ketuvim.
- Jewish festivals include **Rosh Hashanah** (Jewish New Year), **Yom Kippur** (Day of Atonement), Pesach (Passover), **Sukkot** (Festival of Tabernacles), Purim, and Hanukkah (Festival of Lights).
- Jewish boys celebrate **Bar Mitzvah** at age thirteen and Jewish girls celebrate **Bat Mitzvah** at age twelve. From then on, they are responsible for keeping the commandments as set out in the Torah.
- The most important Jewish symbol is the Star of David.
- Jews remember and honour the covenant that God made with his people through Moses.
- Each year, at the Passover Meal, which is called the Seder meal, Jews remember the journey of the Chosen People, led by Moses, through the desert to the Promised Land. Passover, or Pesach, is celebrated in people's homes.
- Jewish people have strict laws around food. For example, they can eat meat that comes from animals that have divided hoofs and chew their cud, such as cows and goats, and they can eat fish that have both fins and scales, such as salmon and cod. Such food, prepared according to strict guidelines, is called kosher food.
- The *Shema* is one of the most important Jewish prayers. Jewish people pray the *Shema* every day.
- Mary and Joseph were Jews and Jesus was raised in the Jewish faith.
- Jesus was familiar with the Jewish scriptures and he often quoted from them when he was teaching people.

THINK ABOUT IT ...

- Do any of the above facts remind you of anything in your own faith?

שנה טובה

Shanah tovah written in Hebrew script

FOR MEMORISATION

Shanah tovah!
(A good year to you!)

RECALL THE STORY: 'JOSH AND ROBERT'S SCHOOL PROJECT'

- What is a **sukkah**, and during which festival is it used?
- Who originally used sukkahs?
- Why does the sukkah have holes in the roof?
- What does the festival of Rosh Hashanah celebrate?
- What is the name of the bread that is eaten during Rosh Hashanah?
- What does the tradition of dipping bread and apples in honey symbolise?
- What happens during Yom Kippur?
- How do Jews wish one another a Happy New Year?

ACTIVITY

- Find out the dates when Rosh Hashanah, Yom Kippur and Sukkot are celebrated this year. They are all celebrated within a few weeks of each other.

JOURNAL EXERCISE

- Jewish people greet one another in the New Year with the Hebrew words *Shanah tovah*, which mean 'A good year to you'. Copy the letters of this greeting as they appear in Hebrew script (see opposite) into your journal and then decorate the page.

AT HOME

THIS WEEK

The children learned about three major festivals of Judaism: Rosh Hashanah, Yom Kippur and Sukkot. These are celebrated both in the synagogue and in Jewish homes. Rosh Hashanah is a two-day festival that celebrates the beginning of the Jewish New Year. Yom Kippur is a day of fasting and making amends for wrongdoing; it is the holiest day of the Jewish year. During the Feast of Sukkot, a tent-like structure called a *sukkah* is set up in the back garden of Jewish homes to remind the family of how the Israelites wandered in the wilderness for forty years and of God's constant presence with them.

Read the Jewish prayer, the *Shema*, together. Jewish people pray this prayer every day.

> Hear, O Israel: The Lord is our God, the Lord alone. You shall love the Lord your God with all your heart, with all your soul and with all your might. Keep these words that I am commanding you today in your heart. Recite them to your children and talk about them when you are at home and when you are away, when you lie down and when you rise. Bind them as a sign on your hand, fix them as an emblem on your forehead, and write them on the doorposts of your houses and upon your gates.

DID YOU KNOW?

During the Feast of Sukkot, which lasts for about a week, Jewish families eat and sleep in a sukkah (when the weather is good enough).

TIME TOGETHER

Chat Together
Tell your parent or guardian what you learned about Rosh Hashanah, Yom Kippur and Sukkot. Chat about the religious festivals that you celebrate in your home, and how you mark them.

Respond and Share
Choose one religious festival that you celebrate with your family. Write about what you do at home and/or in your local church on that day. Share what you have written with your parent or guardian.

Be Curious
Find out more about the three festivals of Rosh Hashanah, Yom Kippur and Sukkot, either by talking to someone you know who is Jewish, or by researching them in books or online.

THIS WEEK IN SCHOOL

You are invited to think about:

- The Jewish Seder meal and how it relates to the time the Israelites spent in slavery in Egypt

KEY WORDS

Plague: An unwelcome outbreak of something unpleasant, such as a disease or an infestation of insects or animals.

Seder meal: A special meal during which Jews remember how their ancestors escaped from slavery in Egypt to freedom in the Promised Land. The Seder meal is central to the Jewish celebration of Pesach, or Passover.

(SEASONAL/ADDITIONAL) LESSON 6: JUDAISM (II)

Pesach (Passover) and the Seder Meal

The festival of Pesach (Passover) is an important festival in the Jewish calendar.

The Story of the Passover

Moses lived in Midian, where he was a shepherd. One day he saw a very strange sight – a bush was on fire, yet the bush was not being burned by the flames. Then Moses heard the voice of God speaking to him. God said, 'Go to Egypt and tell the Pharaoh to let my people go.' At this time the Israelites, the ancestors of the Jewish people, were in slavery in Egypt.

So Moses and his brother Aaron went before the Pharaoh and demanded that he let the Israelites go, but the Pharaoh just laughed and refused. Moses and Aaron threatened the Pharaoh with ten terrible **plagues** from God if he didn't listen to the command that had come from God to free the Israelites.

God sent nine plagues – blood, frogs, lice, wild animals, sick animals, boils, hail, locusts, darkness. But the Pharaoh still would not allow the Israelites to go free. God told Moses that the Israelites should sacrifice a lamb and mark their doorposts with the lamb's blood so that the 'Angel of Death' who would be coming would 'pass over' their houses and spare them from the tenth plague. Then God sent the tenth plague. That night the Angel of Death entered the homes of the Egyptians and all the firstborn children of the Egyptians were killed.

The next morning Moses led his people on their journey, but when they reached the Red Sea they were trapped. The Egyptian army was behind them and they had nowhere to go. Then God told Moses to stretch his arm out over the water, and, miraculously, the waters parted and the Israelites were able to walk through on dry land. However, as soon as the Egyptians tried to follow them, they were swallowed up by the roaring waters.

This is what Jewish people celebrate at Pesach, or Passover – the freeing of the Israelites from slavery in Egypt and the saving of their firstborn children from death.

- What did Moses hear the voice saying from the burning bush?
- Who accompanied Moses when he went to the Pharaoh to ask him to let the Israelites go?
- What happened when the Pharaoh refused to free the Israelites?
- What instructions did Moses pass on to the people from God about the Angel of Death, and about what they should do to protect their families?
- Who was killed by the Angel of Death and who was spared?
- Who led the Israelites across the Red Sea?
- When do the Jewish people celebrate these events?

JOURNAL EXERCISE

- Imagine you are one of the Israelites who escaped from Egypt that night, under the leadership of Moses. Write a diary entry in your Religious Education journal, describing your feelings.

THE SEDER MEAL

Every year Jews celebrate a special Passover meal, known as a **Seder meal**, to remember how their ancestors escaped from Egypt to freedom in the Promised Land.

At the Seder meal, a large plate is placed in the middle of the table. This plate has different kinds of food on it, and each food is a symbol of something that happened to the Israelites before they eventually found freedom in the Promised Land.

A lamb shankbone: The lamb bone represents the lamb the Israelites sacrificed as their special Passover offering. It reminds those gathered at the Seder meal of the first Passover meal, when their ancestors killed a lamb for the meal, before smearing their doors with the blood of the lamb, as God had asked, so that the Angel of Death would 'pass over' their homes and their firstborn children would be spared.

Haroset: Haroset is a sweet salad of apples, nuts, wine and cinnamon. The appearance of this food represents the mortar used by the Israelite slaves to make bricks, from which they built monuments for the Pharaoh. The sweetness represents the sweetness of freedom.

Parsley: The parsley is a symbol of the coming of spring and the flourishing of the Israelites.

Lettuce: The bitterness of the lettuce symbolises the hardship experienced by the slaves in Egypt.

Horseradish: The bitterness of the horseradish symbolises the bitterness of slavery.

Boiled egg: The egg symbolises the circle of life, springtime and renewal.

Matzah: The flat, unleavened bread eaten by the slaves as they fled from Egypt.

Saltwater: Representing the tears and sweat of enslavement.

Wine: Wine is also drunk by the adults at the Seder meal. It is seen as a symbol of freedom.

THIS WEEK

The children learned that, every year during the festival of Pesach, Jewish families celebrate a special Passover meal called the Seder meal. This meal recalls how their ancestors, the Israelites, escaped from Egypt to freedom in the Promised Land. Particular foods are eaten during the Seder meal, each of which has deep symbolic meaning.

Pray together this prayer, which Jews say after the Seder meal:

Grace after the Seder Meal

Blessed are You, Lord our God, King of the Universe, who sustains the entire world with goodness, grace, loving kindness and compassion.
He gives bread to all, for His grace is everlasting.
And in His great goodness we have never lacked anything and we will never be deprived of food for the sake of His great name.
For He is God who provides for all and does good for all and prepares food for all His creatures that He created.
Blessed are You, Lord, who provides for all. Amen.

AT HOME

DID YOU KNOW?

Because Jesus was a Jew, he would have celebrated Passover with his family and friends. The Last Supper was a Passover meal.

TIME TOGETHER

Chat Together

Talk about the special meals your family celebrates. Is there a story behind the food you eat on certain days?

Respond and Share

Write about one special meal that you shared with your family in your Religious Education journal. Include a photo or draw a picture. Share your work with your parent or guardian.

Be Mindful

There are still millions of people all over the world who are treated unfairly by their employers, as the Israelites were in Egypt, and whose families suffer as a result. Be mindful of these people, pray for them, and research the ways you can support charities who try to help them.

Song lyrics

GROW IN LOVE (THEME SONG)

Chorus:
Grow in love of God.
Grow in love of everyone.
Grow in love of God.
Grow in love.

1. God has shown his love for us.
God sent Jesus, his Son.
He told us that to follow him
We must love everyone.

2. The Holy Spirit helps us live,
So we're never alone.
Father, Son and Holy Spirit,
Three persons in one.

3. God has given us the earth,
This lovely place we dwell.
Our world is fragile as it is,
We all must treat it well.

CLOSE TO YOU

1. I watch the sunrise lighting the sky,
Casting its shadows near.
And on this morning, bright though it be,
I feel those shadows near me.

Chorus:
But you are always close to me,
Following all my ways.
May I be always close to you,
Following all your ways, Lord.

2. I watch the sunlight shine through the clouds,
Warming the earth below.
And at the midday, life seems to say:
'I feel your brightness near me.'

BIBLE RAP

1. Are you listening closely 'cause I've got something to say
About a great and mighty book that we're gonna read today?
This book has lots of books inside it, actually seventy-three,
And all the books were written to be read by you and me.
Stories 'bout the life of people long before Christ's birth;
Stories 'bout the life and deeds of Jesus Christ on earth;
Books with wise words there to guide us, helping us to live;
Psalms that praise our Saviour and thank him for what he gives.

Chorus:
The Bible is a library of books,
The Word of God written long ago.
The Bible is a library of books,
Shows the love of God for us all.

2. There's Genesis and Exodus, Leviticus and Zephaniah,
Numbers, Judith, Joshua, Deuteronomy and Jeremiah,
Psalms and Proverbs, Chronicles, Samuel and Nehemiah,
Ezra, Wisdom, Joel and Amos, Ruth, Daniel and Obadiah,
Romans and Corinthians, Galatians and Ephesians,
Timothy and Titus too, and Peter and Philippians,
Revelations, Hebrews, Matthew, Mark and Luke and John.
The last four are the Gospels, now you know them sing along.

SONG FOR A YOUNG PROPHET

Chorus:
Oh the Word of my Lord,
Deep within my being.
Oh the Word of my Lord,
You have filled my mind.

1. Before I formed you in the womb,
I knew you through and through.
I chose you to be mine
Before you left your mother's side.
I called to you my child to be my sign.

2. I know that you are very young,
But I will make you strong.
I will fill you with my Word
And you will travel through the land,
Fulfilling my command which you have learned.

3. And everywhere you are to go,
My hand will follow you.
You will not be alone.
In all the danger that you fear,
You'll find me very near,
Your words my own.

LOVE

1. Love is a mother with a baby at her breast.
   Love is a stranger who is welcomed as a guest.
   Love is a homeland for a lonely refugee.
   Love is a harbour, is a harbour
   where there's shelter from the sea.

Chorus:
This is love, this is love,
This is love, yes, it's love.
This is love, this is love.
This is love, yes, it's love.
This is love.

2. Love is a neighbour holding out a helping hand.
   Love is a language that we all can understand.
   Love is a teardrop as we wave a friend goodbye.
   Love brings us happiness, happiness,
   and love can make us cry.

LAY YOUR HANDS

Chorus:
Lay your hands gently upon us.
Let their touch render your peace.
Let them bring your forgiveness and healing.
Lay your hands, gently lay your hands.

1. You were sent to free the broken hearted.
   You were sent to give sight to the blind.
   You desire to heal all our illness.
   Lay your hands, gently lay your hands.

2. Lord, we come to you through one another.
   Lord, we come to you in all our need.
   Lord, we come to you seeking wholeness.
   Lay your hands, gently lay your hands.

WHO DO YOU SAY THAT I AM?

Chorus:
Who do you say that I am?
Who do you say that I am?
Get to know me better,
Let me get to know you too.
Come to me and follow me
And I will come to you.

1. A teacher? A preacher?
   A prophet? A man? (x 3)
   A carpenter's son when it all began. So ... (*Chorus*)

2. A kind man? A healer?
   A rebel? A Jew? (x 3)
   Calling the world to live like you. So ... (*Chorus*)

3. Example? So perfect?
   A leader? A priest? (x 3)
   Inviting us all to come to your feast. So ... (*Chorus*)

4. Amazing! Messiah!
   You rose from the dead.
   You came here to save us just as you said. So ... (*Chorus*)

THE SUMMONS

1. 'Will you come and follow me if I but call your name?
   Will you go where you don't know and never be the same?
   Will you let my love be shown; will you let my name be known;
   Will you let my life be grown in you and you in me?'

2. 'Will you leave yourself behind if I but call your name?
   Will you care for cruel and kind and never be the same?
   Will you risk the hostile stare should your life attract or scare?
   Will you let me answer prayer in you and you in me?'

3. 'Will you love the "you" you hide if I but call your name?
   Will you quell the fear inside and never be the same?
   Will you use the faith you've found to reshape the world around,
   Through my sight and touch and sound in you and you in me?'

4. Lord, your summons echoes true when you but call my name.
   Let me turn and follow you and never be the same.
   In your company I'll go where your love and footsteps show.
   Thus I'll move and live and grow in you and you in me.

O COME, O COME EMMANUEL

1. O come, O come Emmanuel,
   And ransom captive Israel
   That mourns in lonely exile here
   Until the Son of God appear.

Chorus:
Rejoice, rejoice! Emmanuel
Shall come to you, O Israel.

2. O come, O Wisdom from on high,
   Who ordered all things mightily;
   To us the path of knowledge show
   And teach us in its ways to go.

3. O come, O come, great Lord of might,
   Who to your tribes on Sinai's height
   In ancient times did give the law
   In cloud and majesty and awe.

IN THE BLEAK MIDWINTER

1. In the bleak midwinter, frosty wind made moan,
   Earth stood hard as iron, water like a stone;
   Snow had fallen, snow on snow, snow on snow,
   In the bleak midwinter long ago.

2. Angels and archangels may have gathered there,
   Cherubim and seraphim thronged the air;
   But his mother only, in her maiden bliss,
   Worshipped the beloved with a kiss.

3. What can I give him, poor as I am?
   If I were a shepherd, I would bring a lamb;
   If I were a Wise Man, I would do my part.
   Yet what I can I give him: give my heart.

O COME ALL YE FAITHFUL

1. O come all ye faithful,
   Joyful and triumphant!
   O come ye, O come ye to Bethlehem.
   Come and behold him
   Born the King of Angels.
   O come, let us adore him, (x 3)
   Christ the Lord.

2. Adeste fideles
   Laeti triumphantes,
   Venite, venite in Bethlehem.
   Natum videte,
   Regem angelorum.
   Venite adoremus (x 3)
   Dominum.

3. Sing, choirs of angels, sing in exultation.
   Sing, all ye citizens of Heaven above!
   Glory to God in the highest!
   O come, let us adore him, (x 3)
   Christ the Lord.

HURON CAROL

1. 'Twas in the moon of wintertime,
   When all the birds had fled,
   That mighty Gitchi Manitou
   Sent angel choirs instead.
   Before their light the stars grew dim
   And wandering hunters heard the hymn:
   'Jesus your King is born, Jesus is born,
   In excelsis gloria.'

2. Within a lodge of broken bark
   The tender Babe was found.
   A ragged robe of rabbit skin
   Enwrapp'd his beauty round.
   And as the hunter braves drew nigh,
   The angel song rang loud and high:
   'Jesus your King is born, Jesus is born,
   In excelsis gloria.'

3. O children of the forest free,
   O sons of Manitou,
   The Holy Child of earth and heaven
   Is born today for you.
   Come kneel before the radiant boy,
   Who brings you beauty, peace and joy;
   'Jesus your King is born, Jesus is born,
   In excelsis gloria.'

MAKE A GOOD CHOICE

Chorus:
This world is so confusing,
It's hard to make your way;
Wishing, thinking, wondering
What to do and what to say.
Don't follow like a sheep.
Stand on your own two feet.
Listen to your inside voice,
And make a good choice.

1. Which friends to have, what clothes to wear,
   How to rearrange your hair.
   Which song to sing, where to hang out,
   What to talk to friends about.

2. How to cheer up a friend who's down.
   Stay at home or go to town.

Go to work or college or school.
Study hard or act so cool.

3. Tell the truth and make a stand,
Reach out with a helping hand.
Be yourself or follow the lead.
Christian values are all you need.

MORE THAN JUST

1. More than just our stories, more than what we do.
When we get together there's more to me and you.
More than just some people, more than things we see.
More than we can say in words is there between you and me.

Chorus:
Jesus, you are with us in your new and risen life.
When we meet, you share with us the things we see in signs.
At once God brought the people to a new and promised land.
You're leading us, you're changing us.
You make of us a people and a sign of God's love for all the world.

2. More than water washing, more than bread and wine;
More than just a promise to be faithful for all time;
More than just anointing, more than hands laid on;
In each and every sacrament there's more, more that's going on.

THE BEATITUDES

1. Blessed are the poor in spirit, the kingdom of heaven is theirs. Amen.

2. Blessed are those who mourn, they will be filled with joy. Amen.

3. Blessed are the gentle, they will inherit the land. Amen.

4. Blessed are those who hunger and thirst for justice, the justice of God will be theirs. Amen.

5. Blessed are the merciful, mercy will be shown unto them. Amen.

6. Blessed are the pure in heart, they will come to see God. Amen.

7. Blessed are those who bring peace, they will be called children of God. Amen.

8. Blessed are those who suffer in the cause of right, the kingdom of heaven is theirs. Amen.

GOD HAS GIVEN US THE EARTH

1. God has given us the earth, has given fruits for all.
God has made all living things, all creatures great and small.
We must treasure God's great gift, the planet that we share;
Respect it and protect it and show we really care.
Do not take this world for granted, treat it well, do not destroy
What keeps us all alive.

Chorus:
We must try (We must try)
We must try (We must try)
To protect the world we live in
For all peoples yet to come.
We must try (We must try)
We must try (We must try)
To take what's needed and no more,
So there's enough for everyone.

2. Teach us, Lord, to marvel at the beauty of each thing:
The clear blue crystal water, the sparrow as it sings,
The wolf's cry in the distance and the summer's cooling breeze,
The deep green forest hiding all the many different trees.
Do not take this world for granted, treat it well, do not destroy.

3. Teach us, Lord, respect for all the living things we see:
The vast expansive oceans, the gently humming bee,
The brightness of the snow-capped mountain, eagles soaring high,
The dark rocks that we swim from 'neath a hazy autumn sky.
Do not take this world for granted, treat it well, do not destroy.

THE WOOD OF THE CROSS

This is the wood of the Cross
On which hung the Saviour of the world.
Come let us worship.

WITHOUT SEEING YOU

Chorus:
Without seeing you, we love you;
Without touching you, we embrace;
Without knowing you, we follow;
Without seeing you, we believe.

1. We return to you deep within,
Leave the past to the dust;
Turn to you with tears and fasting;
You are ready to forgive.

2. The sparrow will find a home,
Near to you, O God;
How happy, we who dwell with you,
For ever in your house.

3. For ever we sing to you
Of your goodness, O God;
Proclaiming to all the world
Of your faithfulness and love.

4. For you are our shepherd,
There is nothing that we need;
In green pastures we will find our way,
In waters of peace.

GO TELL EVERYONE

1. God's Spirit is in my heart.
He has called me and set me apart.
This is what I have to do,
What I have to do.

Chorus:
He sent me to bring the Good News to the poor,
Tell prisoners that they are prisoners no more,
Tell blind people that they can see,
And set the downtrodden free,
And go tell everyone
The news that the Kingdom of God has come.
And go tell everyone
The news that God's Kingdom has come.

2. Just as the Father sent me,
So I'm sending you out to be
My witnesses throughout the world,
The whole of the world.

3. Don't worry what you have to say,
Don't worry because on that day
God's Spirit will speak in your heart,
Will speak in your heart.

SPIRIT ANTHEM

1. Come, come brighten this day,
Fire of the Spirit, fire of love.
Come, come, light of our way,
Fire of the Spirit, fire of love.

Chorus:
Holy Spirit, fill us anew;
Fire, wind and breath of God.
Holy Spirit, fill us anew;
Dancing now as we wait for you.

2. Come, come, move in our hearts.
Wind of the Spirit, live in me.
Come, come, move in our world.
Wind of the Spirit, blowing free.

3. Come, come, giver of life;
Breath of the Spirit, breath of God.
Come, come, giver of life;
Breathing within us, life and love.

VENI CREATOR SPIRITUS

1. Veni Creátor Spíritus,
Mentes tuórum vísita:
Imple supérna grátia
Quae tu creásti péctora.

2. Qui díceris Paráclitus,
Altíssimi dónum Dei,
Fons vivus, ignis, cáritas,
Et spiritális únctio.

SPIRIT-FILLED DAY

1. Oh what a Spirit-filled day this is,
What a Spirit-filled day, my Lord.
You have called us each by name,
We give ourselves to you
On this Spirit-filled day.
What a Spirit-filled day, my Lord.
The Spirit gives us what we need
To live our lives each day.

2. The Spirit brings ...
Love, the Spirit lives!
Joy, the Spirit dances!
Peace, the Spirit rests!
Patience, the Spirit waits!
Kindness, the Spirit gives!
Goodness, the Spirit breathes!
Gentleness, the Spirit acts!
Faithfulness, the Spirit lasts!
Self-control, the Spirit cares!
The Spirit cares!
The Spirit cares!

THE SERVANT SONG

1. Will you let me be your servant?
   Let me be as Christ to you?
   Pray that I may have the grace
   To let you be my servant too.

2. We are pilgrims on a journey,
   We are travellers on the road.
   We are here to help each other
   Walk the mile and bear the load.

3. I will hold the Christ light for you
   In the night-time of your fear.
   I will hold my hand out to you,
   Speak the peace you long to hear.

4. I will weep when you are weeping.
   When you laugh, I'll laugh with you.
   I will share your joy and sorrow
   Till we've seen this journey through.

THE WELCOME TABLE

1. We're gonna sit at the welcome table.
   We're gonna sit at the welcome table of the Lord.
   We're gonna sit at the welcome table.
   We're gonna sit at the welcome table of the Lord.

2. Only love 'round that table.
   Only love 'round that table of the Lord.
   Only love 'round that table.
   We're gonna sit at the welcome table of the Lord.

3. Only peace 'round that table.
   Only peace 'round that table of the Lord.
   Only peace 'round that table.
   We're gonna sit at the welcome table of the Lord.

4. Only joy 'round that table.
   Only joy 'round that table of the Lord.
   Only joy 'round that table.
   We're gonna sit at the welcome table of the Lord.

WE COME TO YOUR FEAST

1. We place upon your table a gleaming cloth of white:
   The weaving of our stories, the fabric of our lives;
   The dreams of those before us, the ancient hopeful cries;
   The promise of our future: our needing and our nurture
   Lie here before our eyes.

Chorus:

We come to your feast, we come to your feast:
The young and the old, the frightened, the bold,
the greatest and the least.
We come to your feast, we come to your feast
With the fruit of our lands and the work of our hands.
We come to your feast.

2. We place upon your table a humble loaf of bread:
   The gift of field and hillside, the grain by which we're fed;
   We come to taste the presence of him on whom we feed,
   To strengthen and connect us, to challenge and correct us,
   To love in word and deed.

3. We place upon your table a simple cup of wine:
   The fruit of human labour, the gift of sun and vine;
   We come to taste the presence of him we claim as Lord,
   His dying and his living, his leading and his giving,
   His love in cup outpoured.

JESUS, REMEMBER ME

Jesus, remember me when you come into your kingdom.
Jesus, remember me when you come into your kingdom.

HAIL GLORIOUS SAINT PATRICK

1. Hail glorious Saint Patrick,
   dear saint of our isle,
   On us, your poor children,
   bestow a sweet smile;
   And now you are high in the
   mansions above,
   On Erin's green valleys look
   down in your love.

   On Erin's green valleys, on
   Erin's green valleys,
   On Erin's green valleys look
   down in your love.

2. Bless and defend the sweet
   land of our birth,
   Where shamrock still
   blooms as when you
   were on earth.
   And our hearts shall still burn
   wherever we roam,
   For God and Saint Patrick,
   and our native home.

   For God and Saint Patrick,
   for God and Saint Patrick,
   For God and Saint Patrick,
   and our native home.

CHRIST BE BESIDE ME

1. Christ be beside me,
   Christ be before me,
   Christ be behind me,
   King of my heart.
   Christ be within me,
   Christ be below me,
   Christ be above me,
   Never to part.

2. Christ on my right hand,
   Christ on my left hand,
   Christ all around me,
   Shield in the strife.
   Christ in my sleeping,
   Christ in my sitting,
   Christ in my rising,
   Light of my life.

3. Christ be in all hearts
   Thinking about me.
   Christ be on all tongues
   Telling of me.
   Christ be the vision
   In eyes that see me.
   In ears that hear me,
   Christ ever be.

A MHUIRE MHÁTHAIR

1. A Mhuire Mháthair,
   'Sé seo mo ghuí,
   Go maire Íosa
   Go deo im' chroí.

Chorus:
Ave Maria, mo ghrá Ave,
Is tusa mo mháthair 's
máthair Dé.

2. A Mhuire Mháthair,
   I rith mo shaoil
   Bí liom mar dhídean
   Ar gach aon bhaol.

3. A Mhuire Mháthair,
   'tá lán de ghrást'.
   Go raibh tú taobh liom
   Ar uair mo bháis.

BRING FLOWERS OF THE RAREST

1. Bring flowers of the rarest,
   bring blossoms the
   fairest,
   From garden and woodland
   and hillside and dale.
   Our full hearts are swelling,
   our glad voices telling
   The praise of the loveliest
   flower of the vale.

Chorus:
O Mary, we crown thee with
blossoms today,
Queen of the Angels and
Queen of the May.

O Mary, we crown thee with
blossoms today,
Queen of the Angels and
Queen of the May.

2. Their lady they name thee,
   their mistress proclaim
   thee.
   Ah, grant that thy children
   on earth be as true
   As long as the bowers are
   radiant with flowers,
   As long as the azure shall
   keep its bright hue.

DAYENU

Ilu hotzi, hotzianu,
Hotzianu mimitzrayim,
Hotzianu mimitzrayim
dayenu.
Ilu hotzi, hotzianu,
Hotzianu mimitzrayim,
Hotzianu mimitzrayim
dayenu.

Da, dayenu, da, dayenu, da,
Dayenu, dayenu,
Dayenu, dayenu.
Da, dayenu, da, dayenu, da,
Dayenu, dayenu, dayenu.

Prayers

Sign of the Cross
In the name of the Father,
and of the Son,
and of the Holy Spirit. Amen.

Comhartha na Croise
In ainm an Athar,
agus an Mhic,
agus an Spioraid Naoimh. Áiméan.

Glory be to the Father
Glory be to the Father,
and to the Son,
and to the Holy Spirit;
as it was in the beginning,
is now, and ever shall be,
world without end. Amen.

Glóir don Athair
Glóir don Athair,
agus don Mhac,
agus don Spiorad Naomh,
Mar a bhí ó thús,
mar atá anois
agus mar a bheas go brách,
le saol na saol. Áiméan.

Morning Prayer
Father in heaven, you love me,
You're with me night and day.
I want to love you always
In all I do and say.
I'll try to please you, Father.
Bless me through the day. Amen.

Night Prayer
God, our Father, I come to say
Thank you for your love today.
Thank you for my family,
And all the friends you give to me.
Guard me in the dark of night,
And in the morning send your light.
Amen.

Grace before Meals
Bless us, O God, as we sit together.
Bless the food we eat today.
Bless the hands that made the food.
Bless us, O God. Amen.

Grace after Meals
Thank you, God, for the food we have
eaten.
Thank you, God, for all our friends.
Thank you, God, for everything.
Thank you, God. Amen.

Prayer to Guardian Angel
Angel sent by God to guide me,
Be my light and walk beside me;
Be my guardian and protect me;
On the paths of life direct me. Amen.

Our Father
Our Father, who art in heaven,
hallowed be thy name;
thy kingdom come,
thy will be done
on earth as it is in heaven.
Give us this day our daily bread,
and forgive us our trespasses,
as we forgive those who trespass
against us;
and lead us not into temptation,
but deliver us from evil. Amen.

An Phaidir
Ár nAthair, ata ar neamh,
Go naofar d'ainm,
Go dtaga do ríocht,
Go ndéantar do thoil ar an talamh
Mar a dhéantar ar neamh.
Ár n-arán laethúil tabhair dúinn inniu,
Agus maith dúinn ár bhfiacha,
Mar a mhaithimidne dár bhféichiúna
féin,
Agus ná lig sinn in gcathú,
Ach saor sinn ó olc. Áiméan.

Hail Mary
Hail Mary, full of grace,
the Lord is with thee.
Blessed art thou among women,
and blessed is the fruit of thy womb,
Jesus.
Holy Mary, Mother of God,
pray for us sinners,
now and at the hour of our death.
Amen.

Prayer to the Trinity
Praise to the Father,
Praise to the Son,
Praise to the Spirit,
The Three in One.

Prayers to the Holy Spirit
Holy Spirit, I want to do what is right.
Help me.
Holy Spirit, I want to live like Jesus.
Guide me.
Holy Spirit, I want to pray like Jesus.
Teach me.

Come, Holy Spirit, fill the hearts of
your faithful.
Enkindle in us the fire of your love.
Send forth your Spirit and we shall be
created,
And you shall renew the face of the
earth.

O, God, who has taught the hearts of
the faithful
By the light of the Holy Spirit,
Grant us in the same Spirit to be truly
wise
And ever to rejoice in his consolation,
Through Christ our Lord. Amen.

The Angelus
The angel of the Lord declared unto
Mary ...
And she conceived of the Holy Spirit.
Hail Mary ...
Behold the handmaid of the Lord ...
Be it done unto me according to thy
Word.
Hail Mary ...
And the Word was made flesh ...
And dwelt among us.
Hail Mary ...
Pray for us, O holy Mother of God ...
That we may be made worthy of the
promises of Christ.

Lord,
fill our hearts with your love,
and as you revealed to us by an angel
the coming of your Son as man,
so lead us through his suffering and
death
to the glory of his resurrection,
for he lives and reigns with you and
the Holy Spirit,
one God for ever and ever. Amen.

Care for the Earth
God, our Creator, you have given us
the earth, and the sky and the seas.
Show us how to care for the earth, not
just for today but for ages to come.
Let no plan or work of ours damage
or destroy the beauty of your creation.
Send forth your Spirit to direct us to
care for the earth and all creation.
Amen.

Prayer on Opening the Bible
Bless me, O God, so that
In opening this Bible
I may open my mind and heart
To your Word.
May it nourish me
As it nourished Jesus. Amen.

Prayer on Closing the Bible

Bless me, O God, so that
In closing this Bible
I may enclose your Word
In my heart and in my mind
As Jesus enclosed it in his. Amen.

Apostles' Creed

I believe in God,
the Father almighty,
Creator of heaven and earth,
and in Jesus Christ, his only Son, our Lord,
who was conceived by the Holy Spirit,
born of the Virgin Mary,
suffered under Pontius Pilate,
was crucified, died, and was buried;
he descended into hell;
on the third day he rose again from the dead;
he ascended into heaven,
and is seated at the right hand of God the Father almighty,
from there he will come to judge the living and the dead.

I believe in the Holy Spirit,
the holy catholic Church,
the communion of saints,
the forgiveness of sins,
the resurrection of the body,
and life everlasting. Amen.

Nicene Creed

I believe in one God,
the Father almighty,
maker of heaven and earth,
of all things visible and invisible.

I believe in one Lord Jesus Christ,
the Only Begotten Son of God,
born of the Father before all ages.
God from God, Light from Light,
true God from true God,
begotten, not made, consubstantial with the Father;
through him all things were made.
For us men and for our salvation
he came down from heaven,
and by the Holy Spirit was incarnate of the Virgin Mary,
and became man.

For our sake he was crucified under Pontius Pilate,
he suffered death and was buried,
and rose again on the third day
in accordance with the Scriptures.
He ascended into heaven
and is seated at the right hand of the Father.

He will come again in glory
to judge the living and the dead
and his kingdom will have no end.

I believe in the Holy Spirit, the Lord, the giver of life,
who proceeds from the Father and the Son,
who with the Father and the Son is adored and glorified,
who has spoken through the prophets.

I believe in one, holy, catholic and apostolic Church.
I confess one Baptism for the forgiveness of sins
and I look forward to the resurrection of the dead
and the life of the world to come. Amen.

Benedictus (Song of Zechariah)

Let us praise the Lord, the God of Israel!
He has come to the help of his people and has set them free.
He has provided for us a mighty Saviour,
a descendent of his servant David.
He promised through his holy prophets long ago
that he would save us from our enemies,
from the power of all those who hate us.
He said he would show mercy to our ancestors
and remember his sacred covenant.
With a solemn oath to our ancestor Abraham
he promised to rescue us from our enemies
and allow us to serve him without fear,
so that we might be holy and righteous before him
all the days of our life.

You, my child, will be called a prophet of the Most High God.
You will go ahead of the Lord to prepare his road for him,
to tell his people that they will be saved
by having their sins forgiven.
Our God is merciful and tender.
He will cause the bright dawn of salvation to rise on us
and to shine from heaven on all those who live in the dark shadow of death,
to guide our steps into the path of peace.

The Magnificat

My soul proclaims the greatness of the Lord,
my spirit rejoices in God my Saviour;
for he has looked with favour on his lowly servant,
and from this day all generations will call me blessed.
The Almighty has done great things for me:
holy is his name.
He has mercy on those who fear him in every generation.
He has shown the strength of his arm,
he has scattered the proud in their conceit.
He has cast down the mighty from their thrones,
and has lifted up the lowly.
He has filled the hungry with good things,
and has sent the rich away empty.
He has come to the help of his servant Israel
for he has remembered his promise of mercy,
the promise he made to our fathers,
to Abraham and his children for ever.

The Memorare

Remember, O most gracious Virgin Mary,
that never was it known that anyone
who fled to your protection,
implored your help or sought your
intercession was left unaided.
Inspired with this confidence, I fly unto you,
O Virgin of virgins, my Mother.
To you do I come. Before you I stand, sinful and sorrowful.
O Mother of the Word Incarnate, despise not my petitions,
but in your mercy hear and answer me. Amen.

Prayer for those who have died

Eternal rest grant unto them, O Lord,
and let perpetual light shine upon them. Amen.

Prayer of Commendation

To you, O Lord, we commend the soul of (*name*) your servant;
in the sight of this world he/she is now dead;
in your sight may he/she live for ever.
Forgive whatever sins he/she committed through human weakness
and in your goodness grant him/her everlasting peace.
We ask this through Christ our Lord.
Amen.

St Patrick's Breastplate
Christ be with me,
Christ be beside me,
Christ be before me,
Christ be behind me,
Christ be at my right hand,
Christ be at my left hand,
Christ be with me wherever I go,
Christ be my friend, for ever and ever.
Amen.

Act of Sorrow
O my God, I thank you for loving me.
I am sorry for all my sins; for not loving others and not loving you.
Help me to live like Jesus and not sin again. Amen.

Prayer for Forgiveness
O my God, help me to remember the times when I didn't live as Jesus asked me to.
Help me to be sorry and to try again.
Amen.

Prayer after Forgiveness
O my God, thank you for forgiving me.
Help me to love others.
Help me to live as Jesus asked me to.
Amen.

Prayer before Holy Communion
Lord Jesus, come to me.
Lord Jesus, give me your love.
Lord Jesus, come to me and give me yourself.

Lord Jesus, friend of children, come to me.
Lord Jesus, you are my Lord and my God.
Praise to you, Lord Jesus Christ.
Amen.

Prayer after Holy Communion
Lord Jesus, I love and adore you.
You're a special friend to me.
Welcome, Lord Jesus, O welcome,
Thank you for coming to me.

Thank you, Lord Jesus, O thank you
For giving yourself to me.
Make me strong to show your love
Wherever I may be.

Be near me, Lord Jesus, I ask you to stay
Close by me forever and love me, I pray.
Bless all of us children in your loving care
And bring us to heaven to live with you there.
I'm ready now, Lord Jesus,
to show how much I care.
I'm ready now to give your love
At home and everywhere. Amen.

Journey Prayer
Arise with me in the morning,
Travel with me through each day,
Welcome me on my arrival.
God, be with me all the way. Amen.

Mission Prayer
May all the children
In the world
Share love
Share friendship and live
In the peace
Of God's love
Now and forever.

Ár bPaidir Misiúnta
Go roinne
Gach páiste ar domhan
Grá agus cairdeas,
Agus go maire siad
I síocháin ghrá Dé
Anois agus choíche.

Prayers for the Mass

INTRODUCTORY RITES
Celebrant: In the name of the Father, and of the Son, and of the Holy Spirit.
People: Amen.

Greetings
Celebrant: The grace of our Lord Jesus Christ,
and the love of God,
and the communion of the Holy Spirit
be with you all.
Or
Grace to you and peace from God our Father
and the Lord Jesus Christ.
Or
The Lord be with you.
People: And with your spirit.

Penitential Act A
I confess to almighty God
and to you, my brothers and sisters,
that I have greatly sinned,
in my thoughts and in my words,
in what I have done and in what I have failed to do,
(*striking breast, say*)
through my fault, through my fault,
through my most grievous fault;
(*then continue*)
therefore I ask blessed Mary ever-Virgin,
all the Angels and Saints,
and you, my brothers and sisters,
to pray for me to the Lord our God.

Penitential Act B
Celebrant: Have mercy on us, O Lord.
People: For we have sinned against you.
Celebrant: Show us, O Lord, your mercy.
People: And grant us your salvation.

Lord, Have Mercy
Celebrant: Lord, have mercy.
People: Lord, have mercy.
Celebrant: Christ, have mercy.
People: Christ, have mercy.
Celebrant: Lord, have mercy.
People: Lord, have mercy.

Kyrie Eleison
Celebrant: Kyrie, eleison.
All: Kyrie, eleison.
Celebrant: Christe, eleison.
All: Christe, eleison.

Gloria
Glory to God in the highest,
and on earth peace to people of good will.

We praise you,
we bless you,
we adore you,
we glorify you,
we give you thanks for your great glory,
Lord God, heavenly King,
O God, almighty Father.

Lord Jesus Christ, Only Begotten Son,
Lord God, Lamb of God, Son of the Father,
you take away the sins of the world,
have mercy on us;
you take away the sins of the world,
receive our prayer;
you are seated at the right hand of the Father,
have mercy on us.

For you alone are the Holy One,
you alone are the Lord,
you alone are the Most High,
Jesus Christ,
with the Holy Spirit,
in the glory of God the Father.
Amen.

LITURGY OF THE WORD

After the Readings
Reader: The word of the Lord.
People: Thanks be to God.

Before the Gospel
Reader: The Lord be with you.
People: And with your spirit.
Reader: A reading from the holy Gospel according to (*name*).
People: Glory to you, O Lord.

After the Gospel
Celebrant: The Gospel of the Lord.
People: Praise to you, Lord Jesus Christ.
People: Praise and honour to you Lord Jesus. (*Lenten Season*)

Prayer of the Faithful

Reader: Lord, hear us.
All: Lord, graciously hear us.
Or
Reader: We pray to the Lord.
Response: Lord, hear our prayer.

LITURGY OF THE EUCHARIST

Celebrant: Blessed are you, Lord God of all creation,
for through your goodness we have received
the bread we offer you:
fruit of the earth and work of human hands,
it will become for us the bread of life.
People: Blessed be God for ever.

Celebrant: Blessed are you, Lord God of all creation,
for through your goodness we have received
the wine we offer you:
fruit of the vine and work of human hands,
it will become our spiritual drink.
People: Blessed be God for ever.

Celebrant: Pray, brethren (brothers and sisters),
that my sacrifice and yours
may be acceptable to God,
the almighty Father.
People: May the Lord accept the sacrifice at your hands
for the praise and glory of his name,
for our good
and the good of all his holy Church.

Preface Dialogue

Celebrant: The Lord be with you.
People: And with your spirit.
Celebrant: Lift up your hearts.
People: We lift them up to the Lord.

Celebrant: Let us give thanks to the Lord our God.
People: It is right and just.

Sanctus

Holy, Holy, Holy Lord God of hosts.
Heaven and earth are full of your glory.
Hosanna in the highest.
Blessed is he who comes in the name of the Lord.
Hosanna in the highest

Mystery of Faith (Memorial Acclamation)

Celebrant: The mystery of faith.
People: We proclaim your Death, O Lord,
and profess your Resurrection
until you come again.
Or
When we eat this Bread and drink this Cup,
we proclaim your Death, O Lord,
until you come again.
Or
Save us, Saviour of the world,
for by your Cross and Resurrection
you have set us free.
Or
My Lord and my God.

COMMUNION RITE

The Lord's Prayer

Celebrant: At the Saviour's command
and formed by divine teaching,
we dare to say:
People: Our Father, who art in heaven,
hallowed be thy name;
thy kingdom come,
thy will be done
on earth as it is in heaven.
Give us this day our daily bread,
and forgive us our trespasses,
as we forgive those who trespass against us;
and lead us not into temptation,
but deliver us from evil.
Celebrant: Deliver us, Lord, we pray,
from every evil,
graciously grant peace in our days,
that, by the help of your mercy,
we may be always free from sin
and safe from all distress,
as we await the blessed hope
and the coming of our Saviour, Jesus Christ.
People: For the kingdom,
the power and the glory are yours
now and for ever.

Sign of Peace

Celebrant: The peace of the Lord be with you always.
People: And with your spirit.
Celebrant: Let us offer each other the sign of peace.

Agnus Dei

Lamb of God, you take away the sins of the world,
have mercy on us.
Lamb of God, you take away the sins of the world,
have mercy on us.
Lamb of God, you take away the sins of the world,
grant us peace.

Invitation to Holy Communion

Celebrant: Behold the Lamb of God,
behold him who takes away the sins of the world.
Blessed are those called to the supper of the Lamb.
People: Lord, I am not worthy
that you should enter under my roof,
but only say the word
and my soul shall be healed.

When Receiving Communion

Celebrant: The Body of Christ.
People: Amen.

CONCLUDING RITES

Celebrant: The Lord be with you.
People: And with your spirit.
Celebrant: May almighty God bless you,
the Father, and the Son, and the Holy Spirit.
People: Amen.

Dismissal

Celebrant: Go forth, the Mass is ended.
Or
Go and announce the Gospel of the Lord.
Or
Go in peace, glorifying the Lord by your life.
Or
Go in peace.
People: Thanks be to God.

Acknowledgements

All Scripture quotations taken from *The Catholic Children's Bible*, Saint Mary's Press, Minnesota, adapted from the Good News Translation © 1992 American Bible Society. All rights reserved.

Excerpts from the English translation of *The Roman Missal* © 2010, International Commission on English in the Liturgy Corporation (ICEL); excerpt from the English translation of the Prayer of Commendation from *Order of Christian Funerals* © 1985, ICEL. All rights reserved. Used with permission.

Information on Willie Bermingham and ALONE (pp. 55–56) used with permission of ALONE.

Statements from Bishop Fleming (p. 100), seminarian Thomas Small (p. 102) and Fr Gerry Moore (p. 104) used with permission.

Poems:
'Jeremiah the Prophet' (p. 17), 'The Call' (p. 33), and 'The Voice Within' (p. 53) by Fr Chris O'Donnell. Used with permission.

'Patient People' (p. 41) by Dr Clare Maloney. Used with permission.

'Environmental Change' (p. 69) by Patrick Barrett, from *Feeling the Heat*, Trócaire and Poetry Ireland Poetry Competition 2015. Used with permission.

'Beatitudes' (p. 65), 'The Holy Spirit' (p. 93), and 'All Saints, All Souls' (p. 117) by Christy Kenneally, copyright © Christy Kenneally. Used with permission.

Song lyrics:
'Song for a Young Prophet' by Damian Lundy © 1978 Kevin Mayhew Ltd; 'Close to You' by Colin Murphy and John Glynn © 1976 Kevin Mayhew Ltd; 'Go Tell Everyone' by Hubert Richards @ 1982 Kevin Mayhew Ltd. Reproduced by permission of Kevin Mayhew Ltd (www.kevinmayhew.com).

'Lay Your Hands' by Carey Landry and Jean Kinghorn © 1977, OCP, 5536 NE Hassalo, Portland, OR 97213. All rights reserved. Used with permission.

'Will You Come And Follow Me (The Summons)' from 'Heaven Shall Not Wait' collection (Wild Goose Publications, 1987). Words and arrangement: John L. Bell and Graham Maule, copyright © 1987 WGRG, c/o Iona Community, Glasgow, Scotland. Reproduced by permission. www.wildgoose.scot

'Without Seeing You' by David Haas © 1993 by GIA Publications, Inc. 7404 S. Mason Ave., Chicago, IL 60638, USA • www.giamusic.com • 800.442.138 All rights reserved. Used by permission.

'The Servant Song' by Richard Gillard, copyright © 1977 Universal Music – Brentwood Benson Publ. (ASCAP) (adm. at CapitolCMGPublishing.com). All rights reserved.

'We Come to Your Feast' by Michael Joncas © 1994 by GIA Publications, Inc. 7404 S. Mason Ave., Chicago, IL 60638, USA • www.giamusic.com • 800.442.138 All rights reserved. Used by permission.

'Jesus, Remember Me', music: J. Berthier, copyright © Ateliers et Presses de Taizé, France. Used with permission.

Picture Credits:
p. 36: Photo: Richard Rogusz
p. 66: Photo: Steven Zucker
p. 68: Photo: neneos/Thinkstock
p. 96: Sr Stan photo © The Sanctuary. Willie Bermingham image courtesy of RTÉ Archives
p. 100: © Killala diocese
p. 101: Photo: Erzalibillas
p. 103: Wellcome Collection
p. 104: Irish Dominican Province
p. 108: New York Public Library

Every effort has been made to contact the copyright holders of the material reproduced in *Grow in Love*. If any infringement has occurred, the owners of such copyright are requested to contact the publishers.